Big Carp Legends

Bountyhunter
Publications

First published in 2011
By Bountyhunter Publications
© Bountyhunter Publications 2011

ISBN 978-0-9515127-1-5
Printed in Great Britain

Big Carp Legends

Steve Briggs

**Bountyhunter
Publications**

Contents

Harefields Nelson, a lake record.

Foreword by Rob Maylin

Steve Briggs is more than just a Big Carp legend, he is a carp angling phenomenon. Unlike the majority of carp anglers who predominantly fish their local pools or at most venture down the motorway in search of their chosen quarry, Steve has quite literally made the world his oyster.

Originating in the Kent hotbed of seventies carp angling, he soon stamped his mark on the Darenth Valley, catching four thirties on the first season, a feat unheard of at that time.

In 1986 Steve went to Cassien for the first time, a trip that was to change and shape his life for years to come. One of the pioneers of Lake Cassien, Steve has now fished its hallowed ground for over twenty-five years, waking up most Christmas mornings on its banks with long-time partner, the amazingly beautiful Joan. That first trip saw Steve bank a monster for that time of 61lb 8oz, and Steve's globetrotting carp life had begun.

It's a life that would take him to many foreign shores in pursuit of the world's largest carp: Belgium, Holland on the Twente Canal, Morocco, Portugal, Lake Raduta, South Africa, Rainbow, The St Lawrence, Lake Ontario, Austria, you name it and Steve's fished it. In fact he has caught carp of over 50lbs from five different countries. Being the only angler in the world to do this is his claim to fame.

One of Fox Pool's finest.

But despite all that it is here in England that Steve has achieved his greatest results. From his early successes in Kent, he has been top of his game on many of England's most prestigious venues including The Railway, Harefield, Rodney Meadow, Summerleaze, Colnbrook West, Stockley, Wraysbury and the Mere.

I class myself as being very fortunate to have spent some great times with Steve at several of these venues, not because he is a great angler, which is obvious, but because he is a great guy. You would have thought that all this success might have gone to Steve's head, but far from it. Steve is one of carp angling's really nice guys; his calm temperament and positive attitude combined with a wicked sense of humour makes spending time on the bank with Steve a real pleasure – even more so when he is accompanied by fishing and life partner Joan, who is the sweetest, most lovely person you could ever meet, and a good angler to boot. Truly a match made in heaven.

Multiple winner of the prestigious International Carp Angler of the Year, twice World Champion, Steve has accomplished what very few can aspire to. He has mastered many complex techniques, vastly different to each other – techniques that have allowed this modest angler to become the most successful worldwide angler this country has ever known. An English angler with an awesome reputation across the globe, and within these pages is Steve's life history. Enjoy...

'The Leather' from Johnsons, which Steve kindly netted for me.

Introduction

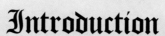

"For people who don't know, the Darenth valley was the centre of English carp fishing in those days"

Going back to the real beginnings; it was my dad that got me fishing years ago, and I can still remember the first fish I ever caught – a minnow from in the stream just up from Horton Kirby, the River Darenth that runs down behind there. I've been back there a few times and had a look, and it's still the same as it was then. There was a little weirpool there, and my Dad tried to get me interested early on. We're talking early 60's here when I was very young, and it was probably mid to late 60's when he actually got me to hold a fishing rod, and then I caught these minnows. I can still remember now seeing the float go under, and not believing how hard these little fish were pulling on the other end. It was the first fish I had caught and I thought, Christ a little fish like that can pull quite hard, and I really enjoyed it. I think my dad was getting a bit fed up because I caught about a hundred minnows and he had to unhook them all for me because I couldn't do it. I can remember him saying, "Yeah, we'll have to move on a bit and teach you to catch some roach or something that doesn't bite as often as minnows do." But it got me hooked from that day, and I thought yeah, I like this, it's good fun.

So I carried on fishing with my dad and fishing various waters, all local stuff. My dad used to be a sheet metal worker, and he worked right next to Brooklands Lake. His factory window actually overlooked the lake, so he was always around fishing anyway, and he loved it, but we could never fish Brooklands Lake because he didn't like spending money. I think it was 25p for a day ticket on Brooklands, and he said, "No, no, we'll go and fish the river over the back because it's free." But I used to enjoy it, catching gudgeon and things like that, and then it moved on a little bit. The first fish that really excited me were pike, as carp were out of the question then; I was too young and they were just a fish that other people caught. So pike were the first fish that one, I could probably catch, and two, they were big and they looked awesome, with big teeth and all that. I used to cut out all the pictures in the Anglers Mail and Angling Times, and stick them all over my wall, and I used to wake up looking at all these pike. The River Beult in Kent is where I caught my first pike, on a Dartford District Angling and Preservation Society water, and they are still going now. They had this bit of river down in Kent; we went down there and I remember fishing little live baits on a pike bung, and I caught two pike. They were the first pike I had ever caught in my life, and that was it, I was a pike angler for a few years. I suppose I must have been about eight or nine years old then. This was late 60's, and pike dominated for a few years.

We moved on, and I joined the Dartford Club as a junior. My dad was a member as well, and we used to go down there pike fishing. I always

Pike were the first fish I targeted. These were my first two caught from the River Beult in Kent.

My second carp ever! Captured on June 16th 1974 at Brooklands. Alongside me is Dennis Davies with the biggest of two fish that he landed on opening night.

remember seeing these carp anglers down there; there were always carp anglers through the Darenth Valley. For people who don't know, the Darenth Valley in those days was the centre of English carp fishing. I didn't know the people, but it was the start of the protein bait era, and there were people like Fred Wilton, Bob Morris, and Gerry Savage. They were all older than me and I didn't know them, but these were the people who were fishing the lakes when I was fishing there. Every now and then I would see them catch a carp, and I'd go up and have a look and they seemed like huge fish to me, but I'm talking about those days, whereas they're little tiddlers now. They were probably mid- to upper-doubles, but by English standards, they were quite big. Brooklands and Sutton were actually big fish waters in those days, and it was a long time before I got my head round actually trying to catch one of those, just because to me, it was out of my league. I could catch pike, but I saw what these guys were using, all these special paste baits and things like that, and I just didn't have a clue what they were.

I think the first time I actually cast a bait at a carp was down at Sutton Lakes. I could see all these fish feeding; it must have been a hot summer, as the water was very low, and I just remember seeing all these bubbles and tails waving out of the water. I didn't have any bait; all I could find were these swan mussels, so I tied a swan mussel on, or hooked it on, cast at these

Brooklands in the mid-1970's. Back then it was one of the country's premier carp waters.

A scaly mirror from the D.D.A.P.P.S. small lake at Sutton-at-Hone.

carp, and just spooked the lot of them basically, but that was my first real attempt at catching a carp. It got to me, as I always liked a challenge, even in those days, and I thought to myself, they're going to be the hardest fish to catch, but I'd love to catch one. My carp fishing really started off differently to most people's because most people you talk to or read about, all started off carp fishing by catching carp either by mistake or on waters where they caught loads of little ones and worked on from there, but I started off on the hard waters. The hard waters at the time were the Darenth Valley, the real pressured waters where carp fishing was really going on so well. I did what I could do at the time, but I only had little ledger rods and things like that, and I was only on a pound a week pocket money as well, and protein baits have always been expensive. They were all hush-hush

First Darenth carp – just a tiddler from the Big Lake in 1975.

recipes, and there were rumours and whispers here and there of what people were using and I've heard of things like casein and Beemax was one of the things that was around in those days, but they were all things that were way out of my league; I couldn't have afforded them, even if I'd known what to do with them. So I was very restricted on what I could use – a pound a week pocket money got me a tin of luncheon meat and a loaf of bread, and that was it.

So I set out to try and catch carp, and this would have been about 1972. You know, I tried really hard during my summer holidays; I was there all the time every day. My dad would drop me off on his way to work down at Brooklands, I would spend the day fishing, and then he would pick me up

A Sutton mirror caught on a piece of anchored crust.

An early Horton Kirby common.

and take me home. I just used to go down there, sometimes see carp on the top, and perhaps lose one. The first year went by and nothing happened, and when you're 12 years old, a year without a carp is like a lifetime, but I was determined to keep going. Towards the end of the second year what really changed was that for Christmas 1973, my dad bought me a set of second hand carp rods. They were only £5 glass rods, but all of a sudden I had a proper carp setup. I had teamed up with this guy who used to fish Brooklands, Don Llewellyn was his name, and he was a real old character. He was quite well known as well because he had been around; he was quite old then, and he had been around carp fishing for years. He actually had a fish from Brooklands listed in the back of Jack Hilton's book, Quest for Carp, in the list of big carp at the time; I think it was 22lb or something like that, so he was quite famous around the lakes for having his name in Jack Hilton's book, and I sort of latched on to him. I thought he was going to teach me how to catch a carp, and I suppose he did; he helped a lot. I used to save him a swim – that's what he got out of me! I used to get there early and save him a swim, and he used to show me a few bits and pieces, but it was all luncheon meat and bread for me – sweetcorn wasn't even around then.

I remember the little sequence of events that led up to my first carp. I had fished on the Sunday with Don Llewellyn in a swim that we call the Sink Swim at Brooklands. I doubled up with him, and we were getting all these bites, which were probably liners at the time thinking about it, but Don caught a 17lb mirror, which again was a big fish then. It was just coming up to half term and I had the next week off. I thought, I know there are fish around here, so I've got to be back down in that swim. Of course I had used all of my luncheon meat, so I said to Don, "Look, I ain't got no bait for the next few days, so if you've got any luncheon meat left, can you leave it here?" There was an old hollow tree behind the swim, and he said, "I'll put it in a bag and I'll stuff it in this hollow tree for you the next morning." So the next morning, my dad dropped me off with a mate from school, Grumps his name was, and we went down to the Sink Swim, looked in the tree, and there was this little bag of luncheon meat he'd left me, which was brilliant.

So cast out and we were sitting there, on a gloomy old day in March, and I remember the bite to this day. The little yellow bottle top sort of went half way up, stopped, dropped back a little bit, and I was going, "Go on my son!" Then it went all the way up to the butt, I struck, and there was a carp on, which, after two years of not catching a carp, was quite an event. I still didn't expect to land it though, and I remember it kiting around and everything. It was a good fight, but I got it in, and I remember that moment when it

My best catch from the early years, including a PB of 18lb 8oz – all caught on worms!

A mid-double mirror from the famous 'Stake Point' swim at Brooklands.

actually went over the drawstring and into the landing net. It was like something that I thought was never going to happen, but it had just happened, if you know what I mean. It was an amazing moment, and it weighed 16lb 4oz, a mirror, and it was fantastic. It had taken me two years of my life to catch; I was only 14, so two years out of 14 was a long time. It was probably the hardest thing I ever did up until that point in my life; it

One of three carp caught one chilly autumn morning when I 'discovered' sweetcorn.

just got the ball rolling, and I was a hardened carp angler then. It was very difficult to compete with all these other guys, because it was the lake where everyone in the country had been; Jack Hilton had been there, and Rod Hutchinson, all with the best baits, and I was trying to compete with luncheon meat. Looking back, it was like float fishing a worm now on Savay – alright, you might catch one, but you're up against it really. But that was what got me going, it really started the ball rolling. It was the only carp I caught that year, because we still had the closed seasons in those days, so since it was March, I only had two weeks left of the season.

So the closed season came, and I planned to do the opening night of the next season. I had never fished a night in my life up until then; it was all just day fishing. My Dad used to drop me off in the morning like I said, and then

Returning a Brooklands mirror caught during the drought of 1976.

pick me up, and I said to him I really wanted to do the first night of the season. My parents weren't too keen, but went along with the idea anyway. I remember walking round Brooklands, and there was an area called the Slaughter House where all the carp seemed to be in the closed season, so that was where I had planned to fish. I remember setting up the day before, June 15th, getting all my gear sorted out, and next door to me was this bloke setting up who I had never seen before. It turned out his name was Dennis Davis, who was one of the real up-and-coming guys in the Darenth Valley at the time, and in later years he went on to fish Fox Pool with Colin Swaden and you know, caught a lot of the big fish there. He was one of the top guys at the time, but I didn't know him yet; he was just a nice guy, and he was friendly enough.

So the first night of the season came and I caught one on my cube of luncheon meat again, which was 8lb 8oz or something like that, and Dennis had two- a 13lb'er and a 19lb 10oz. I remember the weight, 19lb 10oz, because it was huge, 19lb in them days was big, and 20lb really was almost like a 50lb now, that unachievable target. It was great; we had a picture taken together. My dad came down in the morning and took a brace shot of us. I used to pop round and see him a lot; he was a good guy, and he knew a hell of a lot. He didn't tell me any of his baits – none of them did, but he was nice, and he helped. He gave me a few little pointers. I think that was very much how it was in those days. Nowadays in magazines, everyone can't wait to tell you the latest bait, because there are payments involved – if you can tell someone the latest baits, it sells bait for the bait company, you make a few bob, and it's very much a business, money-orientated, but in those days, everyone did everything themselves. If you had a bait, it was one you had formulated yourself and paid for yourself. They were always expensive ingredients, and people didn't want to give them away, so it was all very hush-hush, Secret Squirrel stuff. But he was one of those guys, and Jerry Savage was another one who was down there at the time. I remember he was the first person to actually bring out a protein bait onto the market – Hi-Pro. I remember seeing that in the shops, and I remember it was never that popular with the people round at Brooklands, even though he was a good angler. He caught some big fish, but no one seemed to like him, perhaps because he publicised the fish. They were all frightened that it was going to make Brooklands even busier. It's a bit strange looking back; they were all good guys really, and it was probably just a bit of jealously from most people when I look back and think about it.

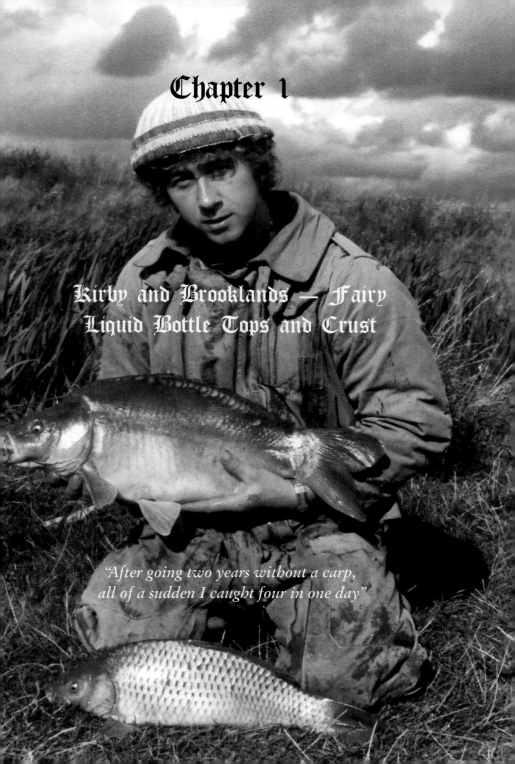

Chapter 1

Kirby and Brooklands — Fairy Liquid Bottle Tops and Crust

"After going two years without a carp, all of a sudden I caught four in one day"

Carp fishing in the Darenth Valley was on the increase, it was all happening down in that area. I moved on to some of the other waters; I fished Horton Kirby that year, and I remember catching four in a day. After going two years without a carp, all of a sudden I caught four in one day! They weren't big, but it was amazing – four in a day. It was like it was going off all the time sort of thing, and I remember this guy coming round and he took a couple of pictures for me and asked if I minded him moving in next door to me. It turned out that the guy's name was Paul Golds. He was about the same age as me, and we ended up teaming up for the next couple of years, and we actually made a good little team. He was a good mate for a while, but I haven't seen him for years now. I don't know what happened to him, but that was my first carp fishing friend if you know what I mean – someone you call a friend who you team up and fish with.

It was a good year; we fished all through the year on Sutton, Brooklands, and Horton Kirby, and I ended up with 24 carp that year, so after taking two years to catch my first one, I then went on and caught 24. They weren't massive, singles through to mid-doubles really, again all on bread and luncheon meat. I remember we came up with this rig down at Horton Kirby that we called the Kirby Rig – a floating crust rig. In the old days we used a big cube of floating crust, a big old stale bit of crust, probably about an inch and a half cube sort of thing, and you cast it out and used the buoyancy of the crust to get it up to the surface. You'd open your bail arm, and the buoyancy of the crust would float it up to the top. Well we soon worked out that the carp were really wary of these big bits of crust, but they would take little bits, but of course, you had to get them up to the surface. So what we did was use something like an early zig rig I suppose, basically a very long link ledger with the link going down to the lead, and a hook length about 4-5ft long with this little bit of crust that was just enough to cover a size 6 hook. We'd cast that out to the middle, it would be on the top straight away, and we caught loads of fish on that. The big ones would just swirl at it or leave it alone, but the little ones would come along and take it, and you know, that was our first bit of inventiveness if you like. It was good; we were catching a few more fish that other people around us, which made us feel quite good at the time.

The following year, we didn't catch so many, but I remember Paul making up his first special bait, and I remember because it was nutmeg. No flavours then; it was actual powdered nutmeg. I don't know what the mix was, but all I remember was he cast out these brown nutmeg baits, and the indicators were going up and down all over the place. Whereas you might sit there for a weekend and get one bite, he was getting all these bites, not necessarily catching the fish, but there was loads of activity. I thought I must nick some of them, so I did. I remember at Horton Kirby, casting one out and waking up in the middle of the night with the reel handle spinning round, because I didn't have alarms in those days. I caught this carp and I remember walking round, showing it to Paul, and saying, "Look at that, my first carp on the special bait, thanks for the bait." He didn't even know I had nicked it I don't think, but that's what mates are for!

It was great stuff in those days; we had to do everything ourselves because there weren't magazines around to tell you how to do things, but there was a couple of books. I remember Jim Gibbinson's first book, Carp – I saved up out of my pocket money, went and bought that, and he sort of told you how to use crust, which was what we were doing anyway. So everything we used and everything we had, we had to do ourselves; the indicators were Fairy Liquid bottle tops, and it was quite funny even then because to be a proper trendy carp angler, you had to have yellow bottle tops. If you had red ones, well, you wouldn't even talk to them if you saw someone with red bottle tops because every shop you went into, all the bottle tops were red and they were easy to find. But I remember Sunlight washing up liquid came out; they had yellow tops, and they were the ones to have. It was just a yellow bottle top, but you had to have it. So we used to go round the supermarkets and nick all the tops off the bottles because we couldn't afford to buy the bottle, so yeah, that was it, a trendy carp angler even then.

As I said, my dad had bought me my fibreglass rods but I used to break them down, take the rings off them and remake them all myself – varnish them and all that. I must have done them four or five times whereas people don't do that now; you get them custom made or whatever, but like I say, we did it all ourselves then. It was all part of the fun, I loved doing it, and I suppose in a way, it sums up the early part of my fishing, because we come to the next season now, which was actually the 77 season. I was still fishing, but I remember it was a big upheaval; I had just left school and my mum and dad wanted to move to Burton-on-Trent. I thought Christ, Burton on Trent – it was like moving to Timbuktu because to someone who had lived in Dartford all his life, it was another country. I thought Christ, I've got all my mates here, my fishing and all that – I ain't going to Burton on Trent. They said, "Well, we're going," and I thought, well I'm not, so I left home. Looking back, I had no doubts in my mind that that was what I was doing, but I was only 16, I had just left school and I left home. I mean, I coped alright, but it was obviously very difficult. I had to find a job and somewhere to live and all that, and of course fishing went out the window. I didn't even

Fibre glass rods, Mitchell 300 reels, yellow bottle top indicators – and no alarms yet!

The result of a night's work with the maple syrup boilies.

know where I would be living from one week to the next, so there was no chance whatsoever of carting round a load of fishing gear and all that. And of course, there were girls around, and when you're 16, do you want to look at a nice girl or a carp? We've all been there, but you can only do so much with the carp can't you?

So the fishing went out the window properly for about two maybe almost three years, but I did still go a few times in between all that time. I moved around, did various things, then met a girl that I sort of settled down with a bit more, and you know, my thoughts started to switch back to a bit of fishing again, like they do once you've got a little bit more security and a roof over your head. One of the guys I used to go to the pub drinking with, said "I'm doing the odd night here and there down at Brooklands, why don't you come down and do a night with us?." So I thought yeah, that sounds good. So I did a few odd overnighters with him, and I remember one morning getting this run and hooking this fish, and thinking that feels good. I got it in and well there was good and bad news to it. The good news was it was one of the biggest fish in the lake, but the bad news was that it was foul-hooked. I was absolutely gutted, because it was certainly one of the two or three biggest fish in the lake at 27lb 12oz, and it was one of the fish that I had always dreamed of catching that I thought I never would catch. It would have been my first 20lb'er, a personal best, and all that, but it was foul-hooked, and I thought to myself, is there much point in really going fishing because the chances are I might never catch a bigger fish than that. So it was a real high and a low, a real disappointment. I forgot it for a couple of months, but the urge just stays with you, and it stayed with me. I started venturing out a little bit more on my own again, and that was it, before long I was a carp angler again.

I seem to remember one of the things around that time was that I bought myself a moped, a Honda 90. I mean it was horrendous looking back now; it was like an old man's bike, one of those with the leg shields and all that, and everyone took the micky out of me, but it gave me my first bit of independence. My girlfriend at the time hated it, and everything to do with fishing. People used to ring me up to talk about fishing, and she would either put the phone down or say, "There's an angler on the phone for you," or something. She hated it, like they do, but I suppose I sprang it on her a little bit by surprise. But that was it; I was back down to Brooklands doing day sessions again. I'd go down there at first light, probably about 5am, and stay the day or whatever, and it was still quite tough going. I remember one thing that changed then was that a couple of the guys I used to go out drinking with said, "Oh, we've got a mate over in Essex, he's got a little lake he goes

to, and it's got loads of carp in. He wants to know if we'll go over for a day."
So I thought that sounds alright, somewhere different, I'd never fished any
of the other waters. So we went over there, and it was called Bulphan Park.
It wasn't a big lake, about two or three acres I suppose. We spent a day there,
and I caught one. It was only little, about 4-5lb, but there were carp
everywhere, and I remember thinking to myself, this is where I should be
really at the moment. I was struggling away on Brooklands, catching the
odd fish, but not really getting anywhere, and I thought to myself, if I'm
going to learn anything about carp fishing, I need to be somewhere like this
where I can catch a few carp, where they're easier to catch, where there's
more of them, and I suppose I just liked the idea of getting a bit more action
as well then.

So I actually joined the lake, and one of the great things about Bulphan
Park was that it was the first water I knew that didn't have a closed season.
I am sure they were meant to close, but they just left it open to get a bit
more money, and all the time no one came down and said anything – they
just did it. It was on the back of a farm, hidden away, off the road, but it was
brilliant. One of the things I noticed was that the years that I had missed,
even though I had only missed out two or three, were probably the worst
two or three years for me to miss out, because there was so much started in
those two or three years, namely the start of the hair rig. I remember going
back down on those first trips back to Brooklands and seeing people using
peanuts on the hair rig. Like a lot of people, I thought they were having a
laugh; you don't use peanuts for catching carp, you use special baits or
luncheon meat, and as for hair rigs – it's not even on the hook! Then you'd
begin to realise that was the thing to be doing, but I'd missed the start of it.
I had a lot to catch up on, that was the thing, and Bulphan Park was the
place to do it.

What I did was to start fishing the hair and start messing about with my
own baits. This was the first time I'd ever made my own baits; they were
obviously pretty simple – semolina, soya flour, a bit of gluten to hold it
together, and my main secret ingredient, Kellogg's maple syrup. Again it
was in the supermarket; you'd go through all the different bits and pieces,
and Kellogg's maple syrup smelled great, like maple, and I knew maple was
a good flavour, and it was nice and sweet. I started making up boilies with
this stuff, and the first time I used it I caught carp straight away, and well, I
just kept catching them. Every time I went I caught carp, and you know, I
saw other people come down to the lake and they were still using luncheon
meat and maybe catching one or two, but I was catching more on the boilies,
so for me, it was a real step forward. I was making my own boilies, but

starting from scratch. I didn't know where to go or what to do with them; it was just trial and error and it worked; that was the great thing. I remember I was catching carp every time, and my target for that year was to catch a hundred carp. I was only doing probably one night a week then, but some nights I would get one or two, and some nights I might catch five or six if it went well. I tried all different things; it was when the carp bait world was exploding, all the flavours were starting to come out on the market.

I remember Geoff Kemp's was one of the main ones, and I was using a different flavour every week. Mellow Brandy was one of them that I remember back then, and Dairy Cream was lovely. Turkish Delight was one of his main ones, and I loved that too. I used to literally fill the baits with the flavours; I used to use half a bottle because it just smelled great, and I thought the carp would love it. It was an early learning process; if you put too much flavour in, you would catch carp straight away. I used to go down there, cast it out, get one in about an hour and think cor, this is great, and

The fish might not have been massive, but it was an important learning curve that would help in years to come.

then catch nothing after that. I soon realised if you put too much flavour in, you might get one straight away, but after that, it was a bit of a repellent, and so I had to tone it down at bit. I was still using the same bait with the maple syrup, but trying all these different flavours – it was a learning year, a year when I experimented a lot with all these new flavours and ingredients, and you know, I was just loving every minute of it. I used to go over there every Friday after work, do the night, catch a few, and I got my hundred carp. It was in the winter sometime, probably January or February, and I remember smoking a cigar that I had taken down. I'd saved this cigar all year, because that was to be my celebration for getting my hundredth carp, and I remember sitting there puffing away on this cigar, coughing my lungs up, but you know, I'd won, and that was a big landmark achievement for me. It was good.

So you know, Bulphan Park at the time, looking back, was a very important year. I'd needed to learn more, and the only way I was going to learn was by catching more carp and trying different things. Bulphan Park was one water where I could do that, and you know after that year, I probably fished it on and off for a couple of years, but that was my one solid year on there, and after that, I was full of confidence in what I was doing, and wanted to get back onto Brooklands. Brooklands to me was still the big fish water in the Darenth Valley, and I wanted to go back there with what I had learned and all that sort of thing.

So I went back to Brooklands, and there were a lot of inventions and innovations going on there in those years. It's not said very often, but fishing with controllers and mixer fishing was invented at Brooklands. I'm pretty sure of that, because even years before, people used to make controllers out of pike floats and candles to use with floating crust to get it out there, and Brooklands was the first place I had ever seen mixers or cat biscuits used, or ever heard of them being used. It was a great way of fishing after floating crust, which was the only way we knew – floating specials and mixer fishing was like particle fishing, but on the surface. Talking about particles, there were people at Brooklands like Dick Caldwell and Paul Gummer who were real inventive anglers in those days. They went on to fish a bit with Rod Hutchinson, and they were the first guys to really concentrate on particle fishing. They had brought through all the different particles, starting off with sweetcorn, which was starting to do the rounds all over the country. I caught some fish on it, but everything was happening at Brooklands, you could see it all unfolding before your eyes, and I had gone back there with high confidence, and I started to catch a few fish.

I had bought a new set of rods, my very first carbon rods, which were

A winter capture that brought me my 100th carp of the year – and the old tank suit was still going strong!

Back at Brooklands late in the season and ready to launch a stringer.

Sportex 11ft 1¾ blanks, and they were ideal for what I wanted. They're a little like barbel rods are now, but in those days, they were authentic carp rods, and again, I bought the blanks and the rings and made them myself. I went down to Brooklands, did a bit of mixer fishing, and I remember seeing this fish cruising along the top. I mean they would have the mixers, but it still wasn't easy. I remember getting a bit frustrated, and cast my controller out, which was my old pike float. This fish was cruising along the top, I wound into it, and the fish just took it. It was almost like I clumsily wound on top of the fish, but for some reason it just took it. It was 26lb, which was a personal best at the time. I had caught my first 20lb'er a few weeks before, a linear at 20lb 4oz, but 26lb was getting to the stage where I had almost caught up to that 27lb'er that was foul-hooked. I thought that with the mixer fishing I would be able to get amongst some of the big fish, and that was one part of the fishing, the other part being moving onto the protein baits. I tried my maple syrup boilies at Brooklands, but I didn't catch anything on them; they didn't like them, which gutted me after catching a hundred carp on them at Bulphan Park.

I thought I was going to slaughter them at Brooklands, but I went down there and never caught a fish on them, so I thought well, I've got to do something else here, and everyone was talking about protein baits, "You've got to have a good protein bait to catch carp." Out of the baits that were on the market then, the one I went for was Geoff Kemp's Ultra Mix. He just seemed to be the main man around at the time, there were a few others but Geoff Kemp's were the ones that were making the headlines if you like, so I bought this little bag, probably about 1lb in weight, and a little bottle of flavour and that would have to last me a month or something. But I do remember using it and catching fish, but all I could do really in those days was to fish single hook baits. There was no way I could bait up with these baits like some people did, because I just couldn't afford it. So I'd have this bag of about 30 boilies, and they would last me the best part of a month. I remember sitting in the corner one day at Brooklands with the wind blowing in, and the carp were there. They used to follow the wind all the time at Brooklands, and I caught three carp that day, all upper doubles, reasonably good fish for those days. The Brooklands fish were lovely fish as well, all big, old, scaly things, the old Galician strain, and they were donkey's years old. I remember these guys coming down, I don't know who they were, but they were interested in what baits I was using, so I showed them this bag. I think I had eight boilies in there, and they couldn't believe it. I said "Well that's it, that's got to last me the rest of the week yet." They said, "You've caught three carp today and you've got a bag of ten boilies?" That was

First 20! A Brooklands linear of 20lb 4oz – the best of three fish that day.

Floater fishing with controllers was invented down at Brooklands and mirrors such as this one just loved a few mixers!

literally all I had, and once I'd used them, I couldn't go fishing until I had saved up for my next bag, but single hook baits were enough to catch them. I found out that if you could find the fish, and if you put a good bait in front of them, you could catch them. I literally used to go down, and put two hook baits on, and even if I caught one, if the bait was still on, I used it again, and that was the bait for that day.

I quickly found out there were loads of different ways of fishing, and loads of different ways of catching fish; you had the mixer fishing and the single hookbait approach, but there were the people who were using the particles. It all started off with peanuts, and then gradually went on to tiger nuts. People would fill the lake in with peanuts and tiger nuts, and I used to watch them and think Christ Almighty, they're putting in tons and tons of bait, and they're only here for a night, but then by the morning, they might have half a dozen carp, and it opened up my eyes a bit. In the early days, Dicky Cauldwell was the main one who did that; he was a serious particle angler. Another guy called Stalker Dave used to fish at Brooklands all the time, and he was either a floater fisherman or a particle angler, that was all he did. If he fished on the top, he'd wander round with a floater rod, mixer fishing, and if he fished on the bottom, he'd fish with peanuts – a very simple approach, but it worked, as he caught loads of carp. It was the thing then that everyone was searching for a new particle, and there were lots of little blinds going on and things like that. People would come up with a new particle, maple peas or something like that, and keep it under their hat. I remember someone using almonds too, and cashews, which cost a fortune, but you could tell from the other side of the lake if they were using cashews because they'd all come down like little helicopters. We'd all pretend to sneeze from the other side of the lake going, "A cashew," and things like that, just to wind them up because they had a little secret.

New particles were the thing that everyone was looking for, and I remember Stalker Dave pulling one of the best little blinds at the time because he was always the man with the particles; he was always the first one to have something new. I remember him coming round, giving us a little nudge, and saying, "I've got a new particle" He went off across the other side of the lake, caught two fish that afternoon, and I remember thinking, Christ, first time out with this new particle, and he's caught two already. Then he caught another two or three, and we were all dying to find out what this particle was, but he just wouldn't tell us. A couple of years later, he came round and said, "That particle I was using, it was peanuts." But looking back, what a great result, because everyone was so busy looking for a new particle, that they forgot about the old ones, and of course peanuts were a brilliant bait. I know they are frowned upon a bit now if they're used to excess and all that, but they were a brilliant bait and still are. So Stalker Dave just went back to peanuts, which no one was using by now; the carp still loved them, and we were all fighting amongst ourselves and creeping round trying to find out what he was using. We'd all used them ourselves anyway and forgotten about them, so that taught us a good lesson there – don't forget a good bait. New baits aren't always the best ones; once a good bait, always a good bait.

The particles were working in my favour, and I particularly remember one time. I had met two brothers when I was fishing Bulphan Park, Ollie and Kevin Wagg from Essex; I haven't seen them for years but they were good old boys. We used to meet up down there and they said they used to fish this lake over in Essex, in Colchester called Layer Pits. I had never heard of it, but they said there were loads of carp in there and he'd seen carp jumping all day, and this that and the other. They said I couldn't get a membership, but I could borrow one of their mates' tickets or something, and I thought, well yeah alright, it sounds good. So one day, I went over to Essex on my little Honda 90, because I still had that. I remember going down the M25 actually on that, because we met up at the Tunnel and he said "Right, follow me down." I had to flash him and tell him I was a learner, and that I wasn't meant to be on a motorway on a Honda 90, and he said, "Well, we're on it now, what are we going to do?" So I said, "We'll better keep going and just hope for the best." So that was my first bit of law breaking I suppose, on the motorway. But we got there safely anyway.

We pulled in the gate, and the car park was up high and it had bushes all around so you couldn't see the lake. It was early in the morning, and I remember Ollie going over to the bushes, looking over, and calling me, saying "Here, come and have a look at this." I remember looking over the bushes at the lake, and I have never seen a sight like it; there were carp jumping everywhere from one end of the lake to the other. I have never seen so many carp out of the water at the same time; there were hundreds and hundreds of them, and I thought, Christ, this is going to be alright. So there was a few things happening around that time, as I was saying to you earlier. It was the time when Zen and Mick Lindsell were fishing there. I didn't know Zen or anything like that, but he was a very inventive angler. I remember this guy getting these rods out of his car, it might have been Zen, I don't know, but it was the first time I had seen anti-tangle tubing, and he'd invented it. I remember looking at this tubing on this bloke's line and thinking, Christ, I haven't got a clue what that's for, but it looks good, so I got some tubing from somewhere just to use because it looked good; I

It was a period when I was only fishing short sessions, days or even just afternoons, but that was often enough.

A Layer Pits double. The place was full of carp and the action was like nothing I'd experienced before. This was one of 19 carp that day.

June 16th and an opening day mirror. I'd found the fish a few days before so I knew where I had to be.

didn't really know what it was for then.

Getting back to the story, we walked around to this, not a point, but like a curve at the mouth of a bay sort of thing, which gave the three of us room to fish together. I was in the middle, like piggy in the middle, and there was one on the left and one on the right of me. I had this little spod made up, like a little plastic pod of something or other with a few holes in it, which was to get my peanuts out. I would fill this thing up with about 20 or 30 peanuts I suppose, and I would cast that out on one rod and where it landed, I would cast my hookbait right next to the spod. I think my hookbait was a peanut with perhaps a little bit of cork or something on it. Basically it was one of the early balanced rigs, or a bit of a pop-up. Actually it was probably a pop-up back then, thinking about it, with a bit of cork to hold the peanut up. I think I caught 19 carp that day; I had never known anything like it. The other two were gutted because they had taken me down there, I was stuck in the middle, and I think the one to the left of me blanked, and the other one to the right of me had two. He got the hump so much he ended up moving round the other side of the lake, because every time I cast this little spod out, the rod was going off all the time. It was only a day session, and I landed 19. I lost a few as well, so I probably hooked 25 carp, but that was the difference the old particles could make; they absolutely loved them. None of the fish were big; there were some big carp in Layer Pits, because I remember Zen catching a mid-30mirror or something like that, and commons of around 30lb. They had spawned really heavily years before, and that was where all these little carp had come from. They had all grown on from low to upper doubles I suppose, somewhere in that range, and it was unbelievable, just like being let loose in a sweet shop, if you know what I mean? I'd cast out and it was just going off, I was loving it, and they just wouldn't talk to me in the end, but it was great fun, absolutely great fun.

I suppose the thing I haven't covered too much yet is all the gear we were using in those days really – the rigs and the tackle. It's changed a lot from back then; I mean it had already changed a lot from the 70's when I started through to the early 80's, and you know, most of that gear is unrecognisable today with what we've got now. I suppose I notice it even more being involved with a tackle company. There are loads of tackle companies about now and we're just one of them, but the materials, the gear that we've got at our disposal now is just such a far cry from what we had in those days. As for bedchairs, it was still Argos bedchairs, which were the only thing we had to sleep on. Well, it was either a lilo or an Argos sunlounger. They came in blue or red, and I suppose it was a bit like the old yellow bottle tops from the years before; if you had a red one, you were a bit of a noddy. The blue one was the one to be seen with, because it wasn't so lairy I suppose, but people used to camouflage them all up themselves and spray them. That was what we had to contend with then; it was just before the real tackle revolution, which was just starting to happen then really. Probably the biggest revolution in carp fishing happened around the early 80's. The invention of the hair rig was the major thing that brought so many people into carp fishing. We caught so many more carp, and people who were really struggling to catch carp before then could all of a sudden go down and catch loads, as suddenly carp were really easy to catch, all because of the hair rig.

But there was a lot of things going on then, like hooks for instance. Leading up to that point, there were probably only three or four patterns of hooks that were worth using for carp; you had the old Jack Hiltons, or the O'Shaughnessy salmon hooks that you used to cut off and put a solder blob on, just to have a reasonable strong carp hook, and there were the Au Lion d'Ors, which were French hooks. They were one of the two patterns that had an in-turned point, and they were good hooks. There was another pattern called the Speed Barb, which was a stainless version, and they were one of my old favourites. Then there were the Sundridge Specimen hooks, which were rubbish; everything used to fall off on them, the points were blunt, and it as like using an old paperclip or something. As soon as you bent into a fish, they used to just straighten out, but I used to use them all the same – I didn't know any better in those days. But then the first chemically sharpened hook came onto the market, which was the Kamasan. They were very fine wire hooks, but actually needle-sharp. I remember the first time I saw one, a guy down at Brooklands came round, Chris his name was; he was floater fishing, and he said, "Feel that hook." I felt it; it was like a little needle, and he said, "I've had four carp on that hook today, on that one hook alone." I thought Christ Almighty, he's had four carp on that hook, and it's sharper than all the hooks I had in my rig wallet. That was my first experience of the chemically sharpened hooks, but nowadays, we just take sharp hooks for granted; it's just a matter of which ones you want to use for which rig.

The early 80's were the days when all this was just beginning really, proper hooks really dedicated to carp. We were coming up with all sorts of rigs; it was like an explosion of creativity coming out of everyone, because the hair rig had been invented, and everyone thought there was going to be loads more super rigs, but of course there wasn't, and everyone was just making variations. I used to use this sliding hook link where it was basically two hook lengths, PVA'd up and all that so when the carp picked up the rig, the hook length slid down. It was a load of rubbish when I think back, but I thought I was the nuts using it, and it was all top secret. It didn't really catch me any more carp, but everyone was doing things like that; they were all searching for their own little bit of individuality with hooks and hook lengths. As for leads, a 4oz lead is quite a standard lead for us to use I suppose, but back then 4oz leads were for sea anglers and that was it. I remember going into Bob Morris' the first time I started using 4oz leads, and all we could do was buy the sea leads and convert them. I used to buy these 4oz breakaway leads, clip all the metal bits off, then drill through the middle, and put a bit of tubing in to make them an inline lead. I asked for these 4oz leads and the bloke said, "What are you going to use them for," and I said, "Carp fishing, to hook them properly," and he went right into

I bought some new Hutchy rods and christened them with this 26lb 2oz mirror.

Early 80's setup. I was still on the Mitchell 300's, but at least I'd moved on to the original Optonic alarms.

one. He was a big bloke as well, so I couldn't say too much but he was going nuts, "You're going to rip the carp up – that's not fair," and I thought Jesus Christ, I wish I had never bothered, but that was the sort of reaction people had to 4oz leads on those days.

It was a huge step up in carp fishing gear; it was all getting stronger and bigger and sharper, and everything in carp fishing that you wanted, all of a sudden, someone was starting to make it. The first bed chairs came onto the market, and we were talking about this a little while ago – Kevin Maddocks bed chairs were something like £250-£300, and people bought them. I didn't, because I just couldn't afford them, but people went out and paid £300 for a bed chair, and you know, even now, it seems amazing that they cost that much, but it was obviously people making a few bob out of us. People started to realise that carp fishing was becoming big business; there was a lot more people coming into it, and there was a lot more tackle to be sold. There was an explosion of baits coming onto the market too. Rod Hutchinson had been around donkey's years even then, and he had his own bait company that was quite prolific in those days. I already mentioned Geoff Kemp, but there were a lot of them. John Baker was starting to do his own flavours and all that, and I seem to remember they were very good and well respected.

It wasn't just the tackle either; there was also the shows and the Carp Society magazine, which was the first magazine I remember reading – a whole magazine dedicated to carp fishing; it was brilliant. Before then it was just the odd article that someone might write in a coarse fishing magazine. I remember John Baker writing one on bait that I have still got today, letting out a few secrets on baits and flavours in Coarse Fisherman – I bought that straight away. But yeah, you know, the shows and things like that started, and all of a sudden you could go to a show and meet up with carp anglers. Before that, the only place you would meet them was on the bank. And there were the CAA regional organisations, and the Carp Society, who were in competition with each other. It was the CAA that I first joined I think, because there were a few of the guys fishing down at Brooklands were members, so I thought that was the one to join. I remember walking into my first meeting, which must have been over at Enfield, the one run by Kevin Maddocks. I remember walking up to the door and thinking bloody hell, that's Kevin Maddocks there. This was a bloke that you had only seen in magazines and books, and it was a bit strange to start venturing out into the carp fishing world, which was going from a little localised sort of hobby to a big countrywide thing all of a sudden, and they were exciting times.

Chapter 2
Darenth — Get on the Richworths

"It always had a reputation for being one of the hardest waters in the valley"

I suppose it was in 1984 that I wanted to move on again from Brooklands, as I had really done all that I wanted to do there. The Darenth complex of lakes was right at the end of the Darenth Valley, not far up the road from Brooklands, but it always had a reputation of being some the hardest waters in the valley. There were four lakes there; there was the Big Lake, the Tip Lake, the Long Lake and the Tree Lake. They both had different anglers on them; the Big Lake was more the lake that seemed to be open to everyone, where most people went and fished, certainly the younger guys. The Tip Lake was always known not to have many fish in it, and it had a reputation of being rock hard, so that was where the older, more experienced guys fished. It really interested me though, because I liked the idea of the challenge, so I decided to have a go on the Big Lake. It took me a while to get a ticket, whereas all the other waters I had fished, you literally just turned up on a day ticket or bought your club ticket there and then. Darenth I think was probably the first place that had a waiting list, it was so popular, and it was the exception to the rule in the Darenth Valley because it was the only one that was really fished by people from all around the country. Brooklands had been years earlier, it's fair to say, but that was just a day ticket lake anyway. Darenth was the first place where you had to buy a season ticket, and there were people from all over the place fishing it, not just local people – it was definitely a step up the ladder from the lakes I had been fishing.

I was still on the protein baits then; I had been using the Geoff Kemp ones, and I started to use the Hutchinson protein mixes. I think it was just called High Protein Mix or something, I can't remember. His range of Sense Appeals had just come on the market, so I wasn't using any flavours, I was just using the protein mix and the basic Sense Appeal, and I thought it was a bait that was going to take the place apart really, well not take it apart, but one that was going to catch me fish. I remember the first weekend that I went on there; I forget the name of the swim I fished, but it was quite a nice swim with a bar out in front of it, a nice bit of open water. A guy moved into a little swim next door, next to an island, which didn't have so much water. I got my baits out, and I remember this guy starting to spod out tigers, and I thought right, he's on the particles. I didn't know who he was, but about two hours later, he was still spodding these tigers out, and I was starting to wonder how many he was going to put in. Actually, he was using a little tiny, I remember what it was; it was an Anadin tin. Anadin pills used to come in little tins, and this was a tiny little thing that held about ten or 15 tigers. I later found out that he used it on purpose to get a good spread of tigers rather than putting out a great big cut-down Fairy Liquid bottle,

An early carp from Darenth Big Lake on Hutchinson protein baits.

I caught a few carp from the Big Lake, but my attentions soon turned to the Tip Lake.

Teaming up with Pete Noonan I caught my first 30 from The Gate swim on the Tip Lake early in November.

My first ever brace of 20's in one night from the Rat's Nest, which became a favourite swim of mine.

Winter fishing could be good on the Tip Lake, but we fished through some harsh conditions!

We were all real keenies in those days – but often the rewards were there to be had.

and dump them all in one spot. The trouble was that a bucket of tigers took him about five hours to put out, and by the end I was thinking, Jesus Christ, will you give it a rest, mate? I was getting the right hump. It was getting dark when he stopped, and I was so pleased, and thought now we've actually got a chance of a fish or something.

Next thing I heard was his alarm going off, and I thought Jesus, he's finished all that spodding, and now he's got a run, the jammy git. So I went down and spoke to him, and you know, once I spoke to him, he was quite a nice bloke. His name was Pete Noonan and he went on to be a good friend actually, but this was the first time I had seen him, and the first thing I saw was this fish on the bank. I thought oh, fair enough, he's caught one, well done, so that was a result. I went back to my swim, and I think by the time I had got back there, I heard his alarm going again! By the morning, he had caught loads of fish, and I hadn't caught anything. I thought Jesus Christ, I'd come down with the protein baits expecting the fish to latch onto them straight away, and he was just using a pop-up over all these tigers, and caught loads more than me. I thought, he knows what he's doing. He lived in London, and had fished round the Colne Valley, which was somewhere I had only heard of. I had only read about Savay Lake and a bit about Harefield and Rodney Meadow. They were the waters he was fishing, and he had come down to Darenth Valley to give it a go with his methods, and they just caught loads of fish. We seemed to just get on quite well straight away, whereas he used to wind loads of people up as it goes; he was quite abrupt with what he used to say, which for a little skinny bloke, wasn't the best way forward. Loads of people used to cop the hump with him, but I got on alright with him. I did actually catch one before the end of that weekend by the way, and I remember one of his fish was crapping out all my bait. I knew they were eating it, so all I did was sneak back and cast one down to his area a bit, and I sneaked one out; it was a 17lb'er or something, so at least I got one.

We met up the next weekend again; gradually we started to fish together, and we started to catch a few fish. He was actually a very good angler, probably better than he realised at the time. He was very clear in his thoughts of what he wanted to do, and it seemed to be working, as every weekend he caught fish, and it was good to see what he was doing. At the time I was using Dacron hook lengths – this was just before the time of all the multi-strand and the Kryston hook lengths. They weren't on the market then; you either used Dacron or you used nylon. Well, carp anglers all thought Dacron was better because it was supple and all that, but he was just using nylon. He said he didn't want to be messing about with all that

Dacron, as it just tangled and broke, which was exactly right – that was all it used to do, whereas you cast the nylon out and it was stiff. It just used to sit on the bottom, and it presented a bait perfectly really, and so I moved onto that as well, and it improved my fishing as well.

Another one of the things he moved onto, and which I do give him the credit for, because it made a big difference to my fishing actually, was the Richworth readymades. It was the start of the bait revolution and all that, and Richworth's were the first ones to bring a readymade freezer bait onto the market. It was a funny thing at Darenth, because everyone was into the high protein baits and all that, and there was the sort of thing that everyone hated the idea of ready made baits; you had to be a real novice to go and

Returning Big H, my second 30, caught from the Rat's Nest just before Christmas.

Looking out from the Rat's Nest late December 1985. It looks bleak but the fish still fed.

The fourth 30 of an incredible winter on the Tip Lake – the equally incredible Scar Bar.

buy a bag of baits out of the freezer. I thought that way too, but the thing was, Pete Noonan was going down and catching two or three fish a weekend on the Richworths, and I was struggling to get one. If I could get one I was thinking I was doing well, but he was catching two or three every weekend, so I thought there has to be something in it. But you know, I was a bit stubborn as well, so I didn't latch on to them straight away. But we had some good times; we caught a lot of fish on the Big Lake, but no monsters, none of the biggest fish. I always had it in the back of my mind that I wanted to move onto the Tip Lake because it was the hardest lake, and it had the 30's in there, so I left Pete Noonan on the Big Lake, and I moved onto the Tip Lake.

I think I did about five or six weekends, something like that, and again I was on the Hutchinson baits and different things. There were times when I was on the fish, and I can remember waking up in the night with fish

Frost-covered ground but another 30 on the bank, this time the Pilgrim at 30lb 5oz.

jumping over my baits, thinking I was definitely going to catch one, but I didn't get one, so I was thinking Christ, what am I doing wrong? In the end I thought, I've got to give the Richworths a go; I've got to do it, just to see, Pete was catching them, so I was sure they would work, and Friday afternoon I moved into, it was I think they called it the Silt Bay it was a little swim just down from the famous Booker's Swim. I remember seeing a few carp there, so I knew there were some carp in the area, and I had a single Honey Yucatan boilie on one rig, and three on the other just to try something different. I think after about two hours I lost one on the single Honey Yucatans, and from that moment I got a huge surge of confidence. I went from thinking Christ, what am I going to do, to thinking I've got it; I'm going to catch one. So I baited up with about a couple of hundred of these little Honey Yucatans, and that night I caught a 22lb mirror, my first Tip Lake carp. The Tip Lake was the hardest lake in the Darenth Valley, and I'd caught one on Richworths – what a result! I remember putting it in the sack and running round to the Big Lake, waking Pete Noonan up, and he thought I was trying to mug him. I remember he was screaming like a little girl, and I had to calm him down, saying "No, no, it's me; I've caught one, it's alright, you're safe."

He came round in the morning and photographed it. I mean, the only thing I did differently was I used the Honey Yucatans whereas he was using Tutti-Fruttis – I did my own little thing, but it was Richworths. As soon as I caught that one, Pete wanted to move onto the Tip Lake as well, which was quite good because it was quite a funny atmosphere on the Tip Lake at the time; it was full of these older geezers, and you very much got the impression that it was their lake and they didn't want intruders on there, but we were like intruders. They would come round, but they wouldn't chat to you, they would just look down at you, as if to say, "What are you doing here? You aren't going to catch anything here – shouldn't you be on the Big Lake?"

Looking back it was people like Alan Smith and Mark Summers, and all they were doing was trying to protect their own fishing, which years on, I can understand. They had the Tip Lake to themselves; it had a lot of nice fish in there, and they didn't want it getting out – they didn't want other people on there. But we were both stubborn, and if someone said they didn't want us on there, then sod them; we were going on there anyway. We started to catch a few fish straight away; I remember Pete catching a couple of 20's fishing along the Fence Bank with the Tuttis. I used to like it around the back channel on the far side of the Tip Lake. You had islands in front of you, long islands, and they formed a channel behind them. It was only about

25yds wide, but most people used to leave that alone, as they wanted to fish the main part of the lake. I liked the back channel because it kept you away from all the other anglers – you couldn't see them through the trees, and it was a nice little area to fish, nice close range stuff and I liked all that.

It started to get noticed that we were catching a few fish. I think it was in about September that we started fishing there, and in November, I remember getting down and fishing in the Gate Swim, which was right over in one corner. It was fairy busy, especially at weekends, and I think the Gate Swim was the only swim left on the lake. I got down there before Pete, but we were going to have to double up in that swim, and it was one little corner. I remember one cold, frosty evening; the frost was forming at about 7pm, and I had a bite. I played this fish in, and I remember Pete saying to me before he had even seen it, "You've got your first 30 there," and I thought, God, I hope he's right. We got this fish in and you know, it was 30¼lb, but we didn't recognise it, even though we had seen pictures of the Tip Lake

An early winter brace for myself and Pete Noonan – the Richworths still doing the business.

A young Steve Wade with a good winter mirror on milk protein baits.

fish. Alan Smith was fishing up the bank, so we went and got him, but he
came down and said, "I don't know that one either." It turned out to be a
fish called the Parrot in the end, and I had an idea it was a fish someone had
moved out of the Big Lake, but no one seemed to know it at the time.
Anyway, that was my first 30lb'er, and I think Pete caught one that night as
well, a 15lb common or something.

We were starting to get a reputation, and people were starting to notice
that we were catching fish regularly on a lake where people didn't catch fish
regularly, and they were all trying to find out what we were doing. It was
quite amusing because it was the time when Tim Paisley was starting with
Nutrabaits with Bill Cottam, and they had Hi-Nu-Val as their protein bait.
I do remember that that was the bait that a lot of people were on, and one
of the guys, I think it was Mark Summers, had blanked for 30 days on the
Hi-Nu-Val. He definitely had the hump that we were catching fish; he didn't
like it at all, and they were trying to find out what we were using. Of course
we weren't going to tell them we were using Richworth, because everyone
was slagging them off. It was a perfect scenario for us, because we were using
a bait that no one was ever going to use because they all hated them, and
yet we were catching more fish on them than everyone else was catching on
all the other so-called top quality baits. It was a great little edge at a time
when you could have an edge, because you know, these days it's so much
harder to have an edge, because as soon as you come up with a good bait,
everyone knows what it is seemingly, and everyone is on it. In those days,
we had that full season just on those Richworths; it's almost laughable to
say, but they were a good carp catcher, and that was all we wanted at the
time.

We fished all through the winter, even if it was half frozen, snowing or
whatever. They were proper winters back then, but we carried on fishing
and we carried on catching. Just before Christmas, I caught a fish known as
Big H, which was one of the big three in there, it was a lovely mirror, and
again another 30, just over 30lb, and that was from the Rat's Nest in the
back channel, which became my favourite swim. Just after Christmas, I
caught another one, again in the Rat's Nest. I went back in there, doubled
up with Pete Noonan, and caught The Pilgrim, again one of the fish that
had real history. It had been moved from the Long Lake into the Big Lake I
think, and ended up in the Tip Lake – it was the fish down at Darenth that
had the real history. I remember a few freeze-ups after that where we just
couldn't fish, and then in January I went back, again in the back channel,
but in the Gap Swim, and I caught Scar Bar, which was my fourth 30 of that
season. It was actually the first time anyone in the Darenth Valley had caught

Looking out to a weedy Rat's Nest swim in the summer.

four 30's in a season; it had never been done before. Alan Smith himself had caught three, and I remember he was the one other guy who was catching a lot of fish apart from us. He was doing well, but I caught four 30's, which was amazing for me then. I had gone from fishing the little lakes, onto the Tip Lake, and my first season I had caught four 30's, so I was amazed by that. It was like all the other years had been my apprenticeship, and this was like the start of my real carp fishing if you like, the big time.

Eventually, we couldn't help but tell mates about the Richworths and all that, and the following year, loads of people went on the Tip Lake for the start, and loads of people were using the Richworths. They were good times, and all of a sudden we had a load of mates fishing on the lake with us, but the catches were never quite the same because everyone was on the same bait. They weren't long-term baits; they were quite instant baits, and after a year we'd had the best out of them. But what a brilliant time that was, in fact really, it was one of the most important times of my life, those couple of years. I started on Darenth in, say, 1984, so it was 1984-85 when I had those 30's.

A good mirror from the Dock swim when the weed was really bad.

I enjoyed my time on the Tip Lake immensely; I made some good friends and caught some nice fish.

Chapter 3
Cassien — The Pioneering Days

*"In 1983 I started to hear of a lake across
the Channel in France, Lake Cassien"*

In 1985 I started to hear of a lake across the channel in France, Lake Cassien. I think that the first time people actually went there was 1984, they were Rod Hutchinson, Kevin Maddocks, Mick Hall etc. At the time, it was a place I could only read about; I had no real ambitions to go there, but at the same time, I had just started to drive. I had just passed my test that year and bought my first car, an old mark III Cortina, and it was a real bit of independence. Instead of going on my little bike, I could actually load my car up and go off further afield and do more things.

Now it was about this time that my other girlfriend who had put up with me fishing all these years finally got the hump and did the off. I can't blame her; she put up with it for about four or five years I think, and that was it. Then I started going out with another girl called Mandy, who most of us around at that time knew. She said, "Why don't we go out to Cassien?" I thought, yeah, I quite fancy the idea of that. Before then it was just something I had thought about. I mean to be honest, I had read all about 50's coming out regularly, and I thought no, that just can't be true. I mean England was the centre of the carp fishing world, it always has been, and yet it had only produced one 50lb carp. Chris Yates had caught a 51lb carp from Redmire in 1980 or 1981, and that was it. There was one 50lb carp in existence, and then all of a sudden there was this story about a lake that held loads of them, and you were thinking, it can't be true. But then all of a sudden, pictures started to filter back to prove that people were catching these fish. Then Rod Hutchinson went out there and he caught three 50's, but it wasn't just his fish. It was when Kevin Ellis caught his fish, the 76lb'er, that I thought to myself, I want to catch one like that! I remember people were saying to me, that it wasn't a real carp, it was a freak, and things like that, but I thought, yeah, I'll have it. It sort of excited me; it got me going a bit.

So it was in late September 1986 that I went off to Cassien for the first time with Mandy. There was just the two of us, and it was a proper adventure in those days. I mean I had literally only been driving for about six months. In England if I went two hours up to my mum and dad's, that was an adventure, but this was like the other side of Europe, and it felt like the other side of the world. It was a nightmare journey; I remember everyone said to me, "Before you get to Paris, there is a turning for Lyon, and you've got to take that turning because then you go on the motorway down south." I remember looking up and seeing this sign for Lyon and going past it, and thinking that there would be another one in a minute. But of course there wasn't, and the next minute we were in the centre of Paris, and French drivers are just nutters at the best of times. We saw all the sights; we went round the Le Champs Elysees, the Arc de Triomphe, the Eiffel Tower, and I was pulling my hair out – it was doing my head in. The best thing that could have happened to me was when I went through two red lights and got pulled up by a gendarme. He waved me over and said, "Do you realise you have driven through two red lights?" I never even saw them, and he must have looked at me and thought, he needs help, this bloke. I was so stressed out; it was a nightmare, and I said, "I just need to head towards Lyon," and he pointed me in the right direction.

So we got out of Paris at last, and it took us two days to drive down. I thought we were never going to get there, and as we got closer, I didn't know the right turning to come off for the lake. We came off the motorway at Cannes, which was this place where all the film stars went, and the area was just unbelievable. I had gone from Dartford to Cannes, and the difference was just mind-blowing; all of a sudden you were driving past palm trees and these big boats in the harbour. The sun was beating down; there were all these women walking about like film stars, and there was me in my mark III Cortina, but it was fantastic, and I loved it. We gradually worked our way through all these little roads, and we knew we were getting close to the lake. I just remember driving round this little bend in the road and all of a sudden, there was Cassien, and it was just a fantastic sight; it was the best sight I had ever seen in my life. I had seen loads of pictures, but I never realised it was actually going to look like that in real life. The water just stretched off into the distance, all blue and clear, and the hillsides were green and wooded. I just stopped the car, looked out and thought, wow, this is fantastic. We drove round the mountain roads, which was probably the best way to see Cassien. You can come straight in off the motorway at one end, or you can drive round all the little mountain roads at the other end. Anyway, we drove round the mountain roads, and it was a real atmospheric way to see it for the first time. So we drove all the way round, and came down to this restaurant, Chez Pierre's, which was the famous restaurant where carp anglers went. There were three other ones, but Chez Pierre's was the carp angler's restaurant, and he was the one who welcomed the carp anglers, obviously because they spent loads of money; he was a bit shrewd, old Pierre.

So we pulled in there, and Pierre was such a lovely guy; he came out and sort of welcomed us in. He was always on the lookout for English or Germans, because he knew we didn't speak a word of French. I had picked up what I did speak at school, which wasn't a lot, but he was ready to welcome us, bring us in, and take plenty of money off us. But it was great – all of a sudden I had driven to the other side of Europe, and there was a friendly face, which was just what you needed when you got there. It was the first time I had ever been out of the country, and of course you feel a little bit strange, so Pierre was a friendly face, which was just what we wanted. We had a meal and a few drinks, and we didn't really know where we were going to fish or anything like that. I mean, the lake was massive, compared to what we were fishing back then; I think it's something like 1200 acres. I've fished waters much bigger than that since, but it was the first big water I had seen. I do remember at the time, the people I spoke to had said different things about Cassien. They all said there's plenty of features in the south arm, the west arm is the one you really want to have a go at, but keep away from the north arm because it's really deep, really big. They didn't think the carp ever went in the north arm because it was too deep and they wouldn't feed there. But I've always liked to do things against the trend, and I always used to like to prove things, so I said I wanted to catch one up the north arm – daft really.

So we hired a pedalo, went down the west arm first and had a look, and I thought yeah, this is alright, this will do if we can't find anything else. Then we went up the north arm, and I remember taking a marker rod with me. We stopped half way up the north arm on the right hand side, cast out this marker float, and I got fed up with waiting for it to hit the bottom. I cast out and it was just dropping and dropping, and in the end, the line was straight down off the rod tip. I mean, it's about 100ft deep out there, and I thought Christ Almighty, I know what they mean. I looked around, but a marker float was obviously out of the question, as it would take you a week to find a decent spot. Looking around at the surrounding hills, the side we were on went straight off like a cliff into the water, but the other side shelved off a lot shallower; the banks were a lot flatter, so it made sense that the features under the water would be a lot shallower as well. So we went across to the other side, and I remember seeing two green umbrellas as we were going across further down the bank. There was no one around really, except these two green umbrellas, and a couple of other people around the lake, but we came to this little sandy beach and I felt like Robinson Crusoe. I mean we were miles away from civilization on this little sandy beach; there was no one else going to bother you, and we were like marooned. Once we were there, that was it, and I thought we could be miles from any fish, but it's a good place to chuck a rod out to start with.

So I got my rods together and the Honey Yucatans, which were still the baits, and I chucked them out. After taking two days to drive down there, I thought to myself, I'm knackered, so I had better turn my alarms up a bit so if something happens they're going to wake me up. Well I must have dozed off, because the next thing I knew, I had this screaming one-toner. I never realised how quiet it went at Cassien – it was literally silent there at night, and the noise coming out of this alarm was deafening, but there was nothing on the end. It was a take, but I picked up the rod and struck into nothing. Johnny Allen was fishing in the west arm; we're talking probably three quarters of a mile away. I bumped into him a couple of days later, and he asked who had had the run up the north arm – he had heard it all that distance away. I was a bit embarrassed about that; I didn't realise how quiet it was. But going back to that first night, the other people who had heard the run were the people fishing under the two umbrellas up the bank. It turned out to be Phil Smith and Joe Taylor who were there with one of their mates, Andy. By then I had re-cast the rod, got back in the bag, and heard these people wandering down the bank. I thought shit, here we go, because you're not meant to be there at night; there was no night fishing. But it was those two and they said, "We heard you have a run, what happened?" I said, "Nothing". So we had a chat, and they went off.

A little while later it went off again, and this time I got it in. I remember thinking to myself, this feels like a good fish, a mid-30 maybe, but it was only 22lb. The power of the fish was unbelievable, and I had caught my first Cassien carp on my first night! I had gone there hoping that I would catch a carp during the trip, and I was going to be there for about a week and a half or two weeks. I thought if I can catch one in that time it would be good, but I caught one straight away. I had lost another one by the morning as well, so I'd had three bites the first night. Phil Smith and Joe Taylor came down and they photographed my fish, and Phil Smith said, "Right, this will do me, I'll fish there." I thought to myself, he's having a laugh, but at the same time, it was a bit of a strange feeling being on there, knowing you weren't meant to be there. There was no camping allowed, and no night fishing allowed, so in a way, it was quite good that they came and fished with us, because we felt secure with a few more people around. In reality though you weren't, and they were just jumping in because they had struggled for a few days. They were just jumping in on the action, which you know, was the bad side of it, but it was alright. So they came down, but nothing happened at all while they were there, and I think Phil Smith and Joe Taylor actually blanked that trip.

It was the first time I had ever come across crayfish, and they eat boilies. I didn't even think about it before then; we didn't have to worry about it, but I was reeling in my little Richworths in the morning, and they were gone. You cast a rod out in the evening, and if you didn't have a bite in the first couple of hours, then you either had to recast, or you just had no bait

In 1986 I went to Cassien for the first time. The beauty of the place just blew me away and my fishing would never be the same from that moment on.

Cassien was so much bigger than anything I'd fished before, but I used simple logic to find a good area in the vast north arm.

left because the crayfish would eat them. It was a problem reeling in because of the snags as well. I was only casting from the bank, and every time I reeled in, I had to reset everything, tie new hook lengths, put new leads on, and it was hard work, really hard work. I do remember Phil Smith was using these jumbo peanuts. I did have some peanuts with me, but he was using these jumbo peanuts, and when he left, there were loads of them scattered all round the bank, and I thought yeah, I'll have them, so I went round picking them all up. I thought they would be brilliant hook baits, because I'd cast them out, and next morning they were still on; the crayfish couldn't eat the peanuts, so I'd found my first crayfish-proof bait.

It was the time of one of the early Paul Regent trips as well, and of course they had to fish the days only and then go back to the hotel at night. The action would just stop before they arrived in the morning, and then it would be dead all day. Nothing would happen during the day at all, and then you would see all these pedalos and boats go back down the lake, the coach would go across the bridge, and then all the fish would start jumping. Once Phil Smith and Joe had gone, I started to get a couple more runs. I caught another 20lb'er and a little common, 10lb or something. A few of the guys on the Regent trip stopped, and I said, "If you want to risk doing a night, come over and stop with us," so they did. There were a few people about, but I don't think they caught. They lost a couple, but by and large, Mandy and I had the north arm to ourselves, and it was just like being cast away on a desert island; I was loving every minute of it. It was just an incredible experience being up there, and to have so much water to myself, that was the thing. I mean my normal fishing was being crammed into a little swim on a little lake and being very restricted, or even getting the last swim that was left. But now, all of a sudden I had hundreds of acres of water to myself, and not only that, but it was lovely water too. You could swim every day, you could sunbathe on the beach, and there were carp out there as well – it was fantastic.

The peanuts made a difference; I remember getting my first run on them, and going out in the boat. Until then, I had tried to play them in from the bank, and I was losing quite a few of them, so we'd hired a boat from Pierre's, which was about a tenner a day or something like that. I thought to myself, well we're not staying in a hotel, so we might as well have a boat instead. So I went out in the boat to play this fish, and I was out there for about half an hour with it. I got it in, and I knew it was bigger than anything I'd caught before. I knew it wasn't monstrous, but I only had Avon scales with me that went up to 32lb – that was how confident I was that I was going to catch something big! I just went there expecting maybe to catch a double or a 20, so I took Avon scales. Anyway, it bottomed out the scales like I thought it would, so all I could do was sack it up and go and find someone in the morning. I rowed about two miles up the lake to these English guys who were down for the day, and I borrowed their scales. One of them came back up with me, and the fish weighed was just over 39lb, a mirror. I remember there were these handfuls of crayfish shells in the sack, because that was what the carp ate naturally. I had never seen fish that ate crayfish before properly, and there were all these crayfish shells and peanuts – two handfuls in the sack. So possibly it might have been close at the 40lb mark when I actually landed it, but it was just over 39lb anyway, and a personal best at the time. It was like the trip was complete; I had gone there and I had caught a fish bigger than I had ever caught before, but I still had a few days left.

A couple of nights later, there were a couple of nights when this group of big fish moved in. I had been for a meal in Pierre's restaurant; we were living on nothing on the bank, just stale bits of bread and all that, so every three days we would treat ourselves. Well in the restaurant were Johnny Allen and Albert Romp with some of the Germans. They were having a right old party with bottles of wine all over the place, and they were all a bit worse for wear, like they normally were every time we saw them in those days. But it was the first time I had met Albert, and I remember he leaned over, wobbled about a bit, and said, "Have you seen the shoal of big'uns yet?" I said, "No, no I haven't," thinking, Christ Almighty, what's he been on? It's the stuff of dreams, old wives tales and that, a shoal of big'uns. Well I went back after that, and this shoal of big'uns turned up in front of me! I knew the first time I saw them, or rather heard them, because it was during the night. I didn't actually get a run, but this fish crashed out and woke me up. In fact when I woke up I thought, that couldn't have been a fish, because the sound it made was just too big, but then I saw the ripples coming into the bank, and I thought, Christ that must be a fish. So I went down on the little beach and sat by my rods, and then there was another fish, and another one, and they were all massive. It's the old story; they sounded like cows falling in, but that's just what they sounded like – I had never heard carp like them jumping. So I got all my rods in, re-baited them, and put them out expectantly, thinking this is it; it's going to go off in a minute. By the time they had stopped jumping, it had started to get light, I was still sitting there waiting for it to go off and it hadn't happened. But the shoal of big'uns did exist, he was right.

The last night of the session was the second night that this shoal was there. Well, I don't know if it was the same shoal of big fish, but there was a group of big fish, and they were jumping. I thought oh, it's probably going to be like the other night; I'm not going to get one. I had fallen asleep, and the next thing I remember was the spool just screaming on one of my reels. I had these little reels, they were Ryobi something or other 3.5's, and they didn't have a baitrunner, but they had a clutch that you could adjust from the back. I just remember waking up and hearing the noise of the clutch going, running down the beach, and in one movement, grabbed the rod and got straight in the boat. That was the thing to do, and I just got towed out into the lake by this fish. If you could get them over deep water before they hit the snags, it was the thing to do, and I remember my line grating and thinking oh God, here we go. Then it came free, and I ended up out over the deep water in the middle, and it was flat calm. It was midnight, and I just had this thing on the end pulling me about all over the place, and it was just an amazing experience, because I was alone in the north arm. There was no one else there, just us two, and it was silent; there was no sound from anywhere, and all I could see was the village up the end of the north arm, and all the little lights twinkling. That was the only light; it was like a Christmas tree up that end, and there was this huge powerful fish on the line that was just fighting so hard. I had never felt power like it, and the fight went on for over half an hour. In the end I got it up to the top, and there was this big creamy flank in the moonlight. I netted it, went back to the bank, and Christ it looked big – certainly bigger than the last fish I'd had. I woke Mandy up and I said, "I think I've got one that might be 45-50lb," and she just said, "I don't believe you," and went back to sleep... cheers.

Anyway I went down and sacked it up, and of course, I had no scales again, so in the morning I had to row all the way down to the west arm, because Phil Smith and Johnny Allen had gone home. The only people I knew on the lake were these German guys, so I rowed down to them, and I mean it was a mile and half row at least. Just as I got round the corner where they were, two of them were out in the boat playing a fish, and they'd already been playing this fish for half and hour as well. The fish just fought incredibly hard, and he said, "Maybe it's the Kevin Ellis fish or a catfish." Anyway, he got it in, and I think it was 47lb-48lb, actually one of the well known Cassien fish, Floppy Tail they used to call it, but it was the first time I had seen it. When we got back to the bank he said his mate had had one as well, and he pointed to a 45lb mirror in the sack and he said, "My other friend has had one as well." I thought Christ Almighty, but didn't say! Still, I said, "Can I borrow your scales?" I shot off, and weighed my fish at 43lb 8oz – my first 40lb fish, and probably to this day one of my favourite carp.

My first Cassien carp caught during my first night on the lake. I had expected to have to wait longer!

My first 40lb carp and one of my most memorable fish. It's impossible to explain the impact that first trip had on me.

People always ask what's your favourite carp, and there have been so many down the years, it's impossible to pick one, but that is definitely one of them. It was my first trip to France, my first 40lb carp, and it just looked massive to me.

So, I did the photographs, and took the scales back, but when I got back, the Germans weren't there. All their gear was there, but they had gone off somewhere, so I just left the scales, but I didn't get to find out what they had caught. A little while later though, I saw the pictures, which were actually used on one of the Tri-Cast adverts in the early years of carbon rods. There was a picture of all three of them; there was the guy with the 45lb'er, and there was this guy in the middle with the 48 that I had seen them land, and the other guy, Dieter Tillenburg, had had a 58lb mirror. I had had a 43lb 8oz, as well, so there were only four of us fishing that night, and we'd all caught fish over 40lb, which was mind-blowing stuff in those days. I had never seen a 40lb carp before, and we were all catching them. But that was it; I had to pack up and go home. I had always said to myself on the lead up to the trip, I love my English fish and I still do, but I wanted to try Cassien, to have a go at France. I thought well, I'm going to go out there, have one trip just to say I'd experienced it, and then get back on with my English

May 1987 I was back at Cassien, and bumped into Pete Jones and Travolta.

fishing. But even driving back home from Cassien I was thinking to myself, Christ this is incredible; it's the best thing I have ever done – everything about it. The fishing was fantastic and the fish were brilliant, but it was the whole atmosphere, the scenery, where it was, and the people – a great experience.

I got back to Darenth, saw Pete Noonan, and I said to him, "You've got to have some of that, it's unbelievable." He wasn't too keen first of all, but I showed him the pictures, and he thought, yeah, I do quite fancy some of that. So we planned a trip for May the following year, 1987. In the meantime I had been a naughty boy and had got done for drink driving. I had only been driving six months, but it wasn't just the lakes that were easy to get to in the car; it was the pubs as well. I think it was actually coming back from a wedding, and I got caught outside my house. It was a stupid thing to do, looking back, really stupid, but I'd done it, and the ban was going to start before the next Cassien trip. So I said to Pete, "We're going to have to go in your motor." All he had was a little white Mini van, and half the room in the back of that was taken up with his speakers. He was well into his sounds, and he had made this speaker box himself out of this big wooden box – I mean the van used to shake going down the road. We didn't know how we were going to do it because Mandy went as well, but she had to fly out.

The drive down in the Mini van is a story in itself, because he'd had this 1200 engine put in it that was the absolute nuts. It was really souped-up, but to start it, you had to put a screwdriver through the grill at the front to hold the starter motor together. You needed two people just to drive the thing; one to poke the screwdriver through while the other turned the ignition. I said to Pete before we left, "Get a few spares, because you never know," and he said, "Yeah, yeah," but Pete was the tightest bloke I knew. Before we even got to Paris the fan belt snapped, so I said, "Put the spare one on." He said, "Oh I didn't get one," so we had to get towed into a garage. Then we overheated about five or six times, and just before we got to Cassien, after a two-day trip, we felt the engine sort of lurching a bit. We both felt it, but we didn't say anything to one another, hoping that we didn't really feel it, but it didn't matter if you know what I mean, because we were nearly there. In the end it got us there; we arrived at the lake, and it was pissing with rain. I'd said to Pete, "There are naked women everywhere, and sunshine, and you'll be lying out on the beach." I think he was more impressed by the naked women than the fish; he just wanted to see them, as I don't think he had ever seen a naked woman before, so he was looking forward to that. But it was chucking it down with rain; there was no one there at all, and he said, "It's just like England, this is." Anyway, we decided to have a go at the west arm, as even in those early days we knew that the fish went to the west arm to spawn, so they should be there. I said, "Well, we'll have a go there, and if we can't find them there, we'll go up the north arm where I fished before."

So we went and set up in the start of the west arm, and three days in it was still raining. Nothing had happened whatsoever, but you know I was still confident something was going to happen. It was slow going though, and this guy came up from the spawning bay. He'd been down there for the day, and for some reason, although we didn't know about it, that year they had opened up the spawning bay. Normally you couldn't fish in there, but this year it was open for some reason, and he came back and said, "Oh I've had two 20lb commons down there today." I thought Christ; he's caught fish. So the first thing we did after he'd gone was to get in the boat, rowed down to the spawning bay for a look, and sure enough, there was a place we could fish from. So we thought right, if nothing happens tonight, tomorrow morning that's where we are going. Needless to say, nothing happened, so we went down to the spawning bay. We had loads of bait left; we had the Richworths and we had the peanuts. We were well loaded up with peanuts, because we knew they were going to work, but we'd also made up our own hookbaits. I'd told Pete about all the problems we had with the crayfish, so we decided to make up these big rock hard hookbaits, which was from only a basic 50:50 mix. I remember I used Rod Hutchinson's cream flavour, but I can't remember what Pete used; it might have been maple cream, the new flavour on the scene then. So, we made up these hookbaits that were about probably 30-35mm diameter, great big things. The way of making hard hookbaits to us was just to boil them for a lot longer. So, we were well equipped bait-wise, and we just needed to get on the fish.

So we got into the spawning bay, set up there, and the first night I remember we were fishing across to these reeds right in the edge. It was only about 3ft deep, so I didn't think we were going to get big fish there, but I thought well, we're going to catch something here, expecting small commons or whatever. But that first night I caught a mirror of about 28lb. I couldn't find my scales, so we put it in the sack, and I thought well, I'll find them in the morning and weigh it. We woke up in the morning (nothing else happened that first night), and I looked out and there were two guys fishing from a pedalo across the other side of the bay. We looked through the binoculars, and thought it was a bit strange, but then I realised that I recognised one of them. I had met Pete Jones from Brighton on the Tip Lake; we weren't great friends then, but we had met each other, and I looked across and I thought that looks like him sitting in the pedalo across the other side of the bay. I didn't know he was going to be there or anything like that, so I rowed out, and sure enough it was Pete Jones with this bloke Travolta, who we had never met before. I asked him what he'd had and he said, "Well we've had a few fish the last few days, a few small commons and that," and I said, "I've had a mirror about 28lb," which was the biggest fish that we'd heard about in those few days. So they came over for a look, and the fish had got out of the sack! I pulled up this empty sack, and you know, I was sick. It was my first fish of the trip after four or five nights, and it had gone. Pete Noonan said, "Unlucky mate," and Travolta just thought we were winding him up, so you know, it was quite funny. Anyway, it was good to see Pete Jones; he was alright, a good old boy.

Nothing happened during the day as usual, but we were all ready for the next night. Bear in mind I was still only using my 11ft 1¾lb tc Sportex rods here; they were the only rods I had, with my little reels, and we were boating these baits out about 140-150yds to the edge of these reeds where it was about 3ft deep. We'd put the oar down and it was only shallow, but you couldn't see the bottom where the fish had stirred it up I suppose. Pete got the first run the next night, a 24lb mirror, so he had got his first Cassien carp. So we had both caught Cassien carp, 20lb'ers – great, we hadn't blanked! Then about midnight, one of mine went off. I got it away from the reeds, because both fish we had caught had got stuck in the reeds – we'd got them out, but it was a bit of a tussle. This one just came away from the reeds easily though, but we went out in the boat to keep it away from our other lines, as we had three rods out each. I was playing this fish, and it started to feel quite heavy. All of a sudden, it came up and just sort of whooshed on the surface, and Pete said, "Bloody hell, that sounded big." Then it bumped into the boat while I was standing up, and it nearly knocked me off my feet. I thought bloody hell, that's got to be something half decent to do that. It didn't fight that hard, but it felt different to anything else I had ever caught, and as it came up to the net, we could see the side of it, and it looked about 40lb too, maybe as big as the one I had had the other October. We got back to the bank, went to lift it out, and it was the old story – you think the net is snagged on the bottom and all that; you've heard it so many times. Literally, I went to lift the net out and I thought Jesus Christ, what's in here? We put it on the bank and we stood there looking at it, thinking Jesus Christ – the size of it. It was at least two or three times the size of anything I had ever seen in my life, and I was speechless, we all were, just looking at this thing. We put it on the scales; it was 61lb 8oz, and I remember we were jumping up and down. We put the fish in the sack, got the beers out, and I was just blown away by the size of it.

We had a bit of a kip for a few hours, not long, then woke up again and there was the little pedalo back out in the bay with Pete Jones and Travolta in it. We thought Christ, we've got to go and tell them. Well, unbeknown to us while we were asleep, they had turned up early and Travolta had caught a low-30, which at the time was his personal best, his first ever 30lb'er, but he was keeping that as a little wind-up for us. So we went out there and said, "How did you get on?" "Yeah not too bad, how did you get on?" Travolta said, "I've done alright actually, never mind your 28lb'er, I had a 30lb'er. Don't tell me you've had a 50lb'er that's got out the sack." I said, "Well no, it's bigger than that actually, and it's still in the sack." You could see he had been shot down in flames, but they came across anyway, and he brought his little 30lb'er across, which we photographed. Then we got this thing out, and I remember Pete Jones looking at it and saying, "It looks like a hippo without legs." So we called it the Hippo after that. It was just mind-blowing; we sat there, and we had all caught – Pete had his 20lb'er, Travolta had his 30lb'er, and I'd had this 60lb'er! That was my trip done obviously. I put it back, and I'll always remember Pete Noonan turning round, shaking his head and saying, "God, I want one of them." I thought yeah, I can understand how you feel – if it had been him catching it, I would have thought the same. So I said, "All I can do is take your rod, your bait, and drop it on that exact spot. I'm happy; I'll pull away from that spot, so you can go on that spot and see what happens." So that night, I took his bait out, dropped it on the spot, and the next morning he had a 54lb mirror!

So that was like the trip done for both of us; we had both caught fish bigger that we had ever expected. Well, I had actually gone out and bought a set of Nash's 120lb scales before the trip just in case. They did them in two sets, they did a 60lb and a 120lb set, and I remember looking at 60lb thinking, yeah possibly, you never know, but there are fish in there that are bigger than that, so we bought the 120lb set, and you know, I needed them, but only just. We were lucky really because we got in that swim when there was hardly anyone on the lake, but over the next few days it started to get mobbed out with Germans and English. Geoff Shaw had a group on there, and he was coming down every day trying to see what we had caught. There were people asking when we were leaving, so it was getting a bit busy. Eventually we left, and I think Big Bob the Biker took the swim over. There were loads of people that wanted the swim, but he was the biggest; he was a Hell's Angel, and when he said he wanted the swim, you gave it to him. He had all our baits as well, I think. But he was alright, a good old boy he was as it goes.

Then we got back to the car park, and through the whole trip we had

My Cassien mirror of 61lb 8oz from 1987. It was just massive. "A hippo without legs," was how Pete Jones described it.

The day after my 60, Pete Noonan latched in to this monster of 54lb.

forgotten about the Mini van. We got in it and started driving up the road hoping that everything would be better, and this kangarooing started and we thought, oh Jesus Christ. It started getting more and more frequent, and worse and worse, and in the end it was getting so bad that it was literally just jumping all the time. It actually ripped the exhaust off the brackets, which was then dragging along the road, and went through the petrol tank, so we had to stop. It was a Saturday evening, all the garages were shut, and no one wanted to help, so we had to tie the exhaust up with an old rod bag, and stuff the end of it in the petrol tank to stop the petrol running out. So there we were, and it was jumping up and down, sparks everywhere, people were flashing us, and we kept overheating as well. In the end we loosened the cap on the radiator so many times when it was getting red hot that the cap snapped off in my hand and we had no water, so we were flagging down lorries just to fill the radiator up, but that was only lasting about 20 minutes before it would run out again. In the end we got towed into this little garage, and we were there for three days while he welded the petrol cap on the radiator, patched up the tank with filler, and put new brackets on the exhaust pipe. He said, "Yeah, it should be alright now." Well we got back in, and it was just the same; he'd patched it all up, but the kangarooing was still the same, and eventually, it took us five days to get to the ferry.

We got back drove into our road, and there was a welcoming committee – all our mates who had been waiting for us to come home. They were all standing outside cheering as we came down the road, and the exhaust actually fell off and we had to go back and pick it up. That was the last time the car ever went – literally it stopped outside and it died there, but it had got us there, and it was worth its weight in gold. We told everyone about the trip and all that; I mean there was quite a group of people waiting for us. To be honest, I thought we were going to catch fish like that every time we went. I had had made two trips to Cassien by then; on first one I caught a 40lb'er when I wasn't really well equipped, and on the second one I wasn't well equipped either, just a little bit more, and we'd had caught a 50lb'er and a 60lb'er! We thought that was what French carp fishing, and Cassien, was going to be like that all the time, but little did I know at the time that it was actually going to take me 18 years to beat that 60lb PB.

So I suppose it puts into perspective how lucky I was to catch a fish of that size back then, and how we had just got it right that time. We were in the right place at the right time; we got the tactics right, and we caught the fish. But it certainly wasn't going to be like that every time, as we were to find out. It was incredible; it changed my carp fishing life for sure and after that time, it was never going to be the same.

Chapter 4
Johnsons and Fox Pool

"Both were very deep and very weedy, so it was going to be a lot more difficult, I could see from the start, but again I was up for the challenge"

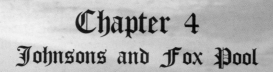

So anyway, after that, we got back and I fished with Pete Noonan a few more times, but I remember that he sort of blew himself out. He lost his job and did a year on Darenth, fishing two weeks on and two days off. He caught loads of fish, but he blew himself out – at around the same time as the Cassien trip. He virtually hung up his rods after that, so I was left in limbo a bit, but Pete Jones was still about. I was still seeing him down at Darenth; we had met up down there and he had pictures of my 60lb'er and all that. We got more and more friendly and started fishing together. He mentioned two lakes; one that he wanted to have a go at and one he had already fished, Johnson's, also a Kent water. He had been down and had had a few little goes on it; I think he and Travolta had both caught a Johnson's carp, and he said how good it was down there – very hard, but very good. The other water we wanted to have a go at was Fox Pool; we had both read about it; a water up in the Colne Valley that was known to hold some very, very good fish, but was very difficult, similar to Johnson's. They were small, deep waters, but very hard.

I suppose at the time it was just what I was looking for; I had caught some good fish, and I was on a bit of a roll I suppose. I had caught some good fish out of Darenth, some good fish out of Cassien; things were going well, and I was looking to move it on a little bit, so we went down to Johnson's. I know the first time I went down there, I didn't fish, but Pete and Travolta took us for a walk round. We bumped into a guy called Richard who had caught the Leather. The Railway Leather was the main fish in the lake, and I think Pete had seen it caught, or he had seen the pictures. Anyway, Richard was there; it's all a bit fuzzy now, but I know that he and his mate were on there, and this guy had already caught the Leather. I think it was the following weekend we fished there, and he brought down pictures to show us. We looked at this leather, and it was fantastic. I don't think I had ever seen a leather that big at the time, as in Darenth and Brooklands the fish were all mirrors or commons, so a 34lb leather was one of the biggest I knew of. It was a very impressive looking fish, so we fancied having a go for it. I think his mate caught one about 23lb that weekend; we blanked, but I enjoyed it. It was a different thing altogether to the waters I had fished previously – very deep, and very weedy. There were quite a few fish in there, but there was a lot more natural food, and it was going to be a lot more difficult, I could see that from the start, but again I was up for the challenge.

To start with I think we fished it from the autumn through to the end, and I didn't catch a fish at all, but the place had got us going, and we fancied a bit more of it. The plan was to do the start of the season; we still had the proper closed seasons in those days. The season started on June 16th and we had a three-month wait until the start of the season. The plan was that Pete Jones and I would do the start on Johnson's with Steve Wade, a guy who we had met on Darenth. He was only a young guy, still at school then, or just finishing school, but a good little angler, and he was alright. A week before the start, Pete and I set up in the Bridge swim, and Wadey set up in the swim above. I went back to work, Pete went back to Brighton, and Wadey stayed on the lake for a week on his own. By the time we turned up for the start, he'd already done a week's session without the rods in the water, poor bloke; I mean he looked ready to go home, and he hadn't even started fishing yet. A week was a long time for a school kid to sit, but he saved our swims, bless him.

We had two different plans of attack; one was with particles, sweetcorn mainly. We knew the fish didn't mind particles, but hemp and tigers had been done, and not many people used sweetcorn, so we fancied giving it a go. You were allowed to use more than two rods on Johnson's, which was unusual back then. Every other water we fished was two rods only, but on Johnson's you could use three or four if you had the licences, so it gave us a chance to try different things. We had one or two on sweetcorn and the other two were on boilies, protein baits or whatever, and we were just making them up on the bank. I remember taking all the ingredients down, buying the eggs up the shop, and we'd just make them up as we went along. I think I was using cinnamon flavouring or something; I forget what they were now, probably our own mix, but I can't even remember. Travolta was there as well.

The first couple of days we didn't have anything. I think Pete had a tench of about 9lb, which was the biggest tench we had ever seen, and Wadey lost a fish, and said, "It wasn't very big; it might have been a tench." That would come back to haunt him a few days later, but the first run was to Travolta. We had thought long and hard about how to catch the fish, as they were so much on the naturals. We thought about the particle approach to compete with, or complement the naturals, and boilies to give them something different. Travolta, with his typical type of idea, said, "Well they've got everything they need in the lake; there's nothing we can possibly give them that will compete, but after you've had a good meal, what would you like? What I like is either a nice dessert or a selection from the cheeseboard." Then he said, "Well, they haven't got that in the lake, but I've got some peaches and cream boilies, and some blue cheese boilies."

It was a load of nonsense, and typical Travolta, but lo and behold on the third morning, it went rattling off, and he caught a 24lb leather. We all went down to look, and it was a lovely fish; I mean they were stunning fish, the

It wasn't too hard to spot the fish and they could often be found in the pads.

They wouldn't always take floaters, but when they did it offered perhaps the best chance.

There were only a few of us fishing the Railway, and the atmosphere was good.

My first Railway carp of 24lb 12oz, which came off the top.

Pete Jones with the fantastic Railway Leather.

It wasn't just the fishing that was hard at Johnson's – sometimes it was difficult just to get there!

Johnson's fish. All the Brooklands fish and all the Darenth fish had a bit of history; they had all been caught quite a few times, and although they were nice fish, you could see they had been caught a few times, but these Johnson's fish all looked brand new. They had hardly ever been caught, and they just looked incredible. They were lovely fish, and so we were well impressed to see Travolta with this fish. God knows how he caught it but he did, and he had to go. He had caught his fish after his weekend, but Pete, Wadey and I were still staying on there for the week. Travolta left, and these two other guys moved in his swim.

Pete had always said that they didn't mind a floater or two if they were in the mood, but they wouldn't have them all the time. I think in the closed season we'd had them going on floaters a few times, and since nothing was happening, we wandered round, and in one corner I saw a couple of fish mooching about. No one was fishing there, so I fired out a few mixers, but nothing seemed to happen, and the fish ignored them, so we went up to chat with the guys who had moved into Travolta's swim, which was the next swim up. We were chatting away to them, and I happened to glance down the bank where I saw this big pair of lips come up and take a mixer, and then another, and then all of a sudden there were a few swirls. They were having them, so I nudged Pete, because I didn't want everyone to know the fish were there, because their swim was further up the bank. I nudged him, and he saw them as well, and we made our excuses, "Better get back to the rods," and all that, and we crept out of the swim and legged it as fast as we could back to the rods.

Pete was the only one who had a controller (I never had a controller), but he didn't have a rod that was suitable for setting up with floater gear and I did, so between us we set up a floater rod. We crept past the swim where the other guys were (they still hadn't noticed the fish), sneaked in, and they were having them big time. There were mouths everywhere, so I got a good cast in, well over the fish, and drew it back. Just as it got to them, a pair of lips came up, and wallop, that was it – I was in straight away in about five seconds. I got that one in, and it was 24lb 12oz, my first Johnson's carp. I was over the moon with that – I had got a carp the opening week of the season, my first Johnson's carp, but there were still loads of fish out there, so it was Pete's turn to have a go, as I'd had my one.

Pete had never floater fished before with mixers or anything like that; he had done a bit of freelining, but it was a bit different to what he had cast out before, what with the long hook length. We used something like 5ft hook length down to two little soaked mixers that were soft, to put on the hook easier. He tried casting that out, and it hit one straight on the back straight away and spooked it. He couldn't get it right at all; he was thrashing the water to a foam and in the end, and all the fish were disappearing. He was casting all over the place, on their heads, on their backs, drawing line across them, and it just wasn't going right. The more he tried to get a good cast in, the more it went wrong, and in the end there was one fish down in the corner that was still having them where these mixers had drifted down into the corner. It was the only one left, so he crept down there, cast, and it was perfect, the best cast he had done, close to the far bank, but enough so he could draw it back, and sure enough this fish came up and took it, and he was in.

My landing net was still back up the bank somewhere, so I legged it up and got it, and by the time I got back, Pete was up to his chest in the lake. The fish had kited up near the trees, and the only thing he could do was jump in the lake, which he did. It was important to get the fish in, so I jumped in next to him with the landing net. It was fighting hard, and as it came closer and closer, I saw it roll on the top, and I knew which fish it was; it was the Leather. I said to Pete, "Go easy mate, you've got plenty of time – it's the Leather," which didn't help matters, but sure enough we got it in, and it was the Leather.

I remember putting it on the mat, and when we went to unhook it, there was another hook length hanging out of is mouth. I thought, Christ, it's been hooked before, and Wadey looked at it and he said, "That's my hook length, and it was. I knew what he was using, so this fish that Wadey had lost at the start was the Leather, and he was gutted. Imagine how he felt; he had sat on the lake for a week without the rods out, got a take, lost it, and then seen the fish landed, and it was the Leather, he could have had the Leather straightaway out of there, but fair play to him. We all went up the pub like you do, and had a drink, and Wadey came up with us, and we all celebrated. It was a good start to the old Johnson's fishing; we had both got off the mark.

It was good to see some of the old guys down there. I remember just when we were photographing Pete with the Leather, Fred Wilton came round. I had never met Fred Wilton before, even though I had always been around that area, growing up with the protein baits, but he was just a name. Anyway, he just happened to turn up in the swim and said, "Oh alright, you've got the Leather," and it was fish he had caught years before. It was just quite a nice little moment, a little moment of proper Kent fishing.

So we'd got off the mark, and I kept trying different things every week. I mean I was still working full time, so I would go back every weekend and I was trying all sorts of things to catch one off the bottom. The thing I was struggling with in those days was the pop-ups, and looking back, what I really needed to do was sort out some decent pop-ups, which I did in the end, but at the time I was trying all sorts of different baits. We were trying different pop-up mixes, and they were rubbish to be honest. To make the old pop-ups we used to put them in the oven, which was all right for the shallower waters like Darenth and all that, as they would stay up most of the night, but in deeper water like Johnson's, after a couple of hours they were just sinking; they just weren't any good.

So I was really struggling, and my second fish came off the top again. It was quite a few weeks later, well into the season, and again there was one of these rare moments where they were all in one corner, and they all started having the mixers after a thunderstorm. I remember a big thunderstorm, and then it all went dark and flat calm, and all of a sudden the fish were there on top, and they were having it. I pulled out of a few, and missed a few, but then all of a sudden I hooked one, got it in, and it was 29lb 10oz, far and away the biggest fish I had ever caught off the top. In fact it is still the biggest fish I have ever caught off the top; I don't do a lot of floater fishing these days, and you know, I have never beaten that one, but at that point, it was an unknown fish. There were a few of the old regulars there; Derek and a few of the other guys, and he came up and photographed it. He showed the pictures to other guys who had fished there, and they all said, "Um, I don't know that one." So that was quite special, but again it was off the top, and I was struggling to get them off the bottom.

We started having a few little dabbles on Fox Pool, and the first time I went up there was in September or October. I fished in the Pier Swim, and nothing happened. I just remember it was quite weird, because we turned up on the Friday evening, and there were loads of cars in the car park, and loads of bivvies around the lake, but there was no one there – the place was deserted – it was like the Mary Celeste. We couldn't work out what was going on, so we set up anyway in the Pier Swim, but I didn't know it was the Pier Swim at the time, but it was empty. The thing I remember about it was that the fish were jumping. I always expected not to see any fish, or

A previously unknown Johnson's mirror of 29lb 10oz, and a surface-caught best for me.

Travolta with one of his Railway carp.

My first session at Fox Pool, set up in the Pier swim.

Looking out on Fox Pool from one of my favourite swims.

Steve Allcott plays the first of his Fox Pool carp.

maybe one or two every few weeks, but these big fish were actually quite active and showing a lot, which was really good. I remember setting up in the evening, listening to them, and then it got to about 11.30pm, and I heard all this noise. It was the Longfield Drinking Team coming back from the pub, and I thought, oh that's where they've all been. I remember someone, I think it was Johnny Allen, shouting across the lake, "There must be some serious carp anglers on here," because there were two of us sitting in our bivvies fishing, and everyone else had been away.

It felt a bit funny because we didn't know anyone there, and the second weekend, we fished adjacent swims on the right hand bank. There was a guy a bit further down; I don't know who he was, but he was in with that sort of crowd, and he didn't seem to really want to speak to us. He was in with that lot, and we were imposing on their little group, so he didn't want to know us. I remember the following morning, waking up about 7am, looking out, and a fish rolled in my swim. I had a bag of Richworths, as I still had a bit of confidence in them, so I reeled in and put one on, cast to this fish, and it just landed in the rings nicely about 50yds out. I made a cup of tea and went up to sit with Pete in the next swim, and we were sitting there having a cup of tea when that rod just blitzed off all of a sudden, a one-toner. It absolutely screamed off, and literally by the time I had run 10yds back to my rods, it had gone through about three weedbeds, and you could see the big trail of bubbles. It was absolutely solid, and I tried for ages to get it out, but I just couldn't move it. I left it a couple of hours, but in the end I just had to pull for a break, as the fish was obviously gone anyway by then.

All of a sudden this bloke who didn't want to know us was in the swim, and he was our best mate. He wanted to find out what we were using, if it was on a boilie or a tiger nut and all that. Then a few of them started to come round, and to be fair, they were all really nice guys. The twins were on there; Nigel and I can't remember the other guy's name; John Holt's friend Ian Booker was on there; Colin Martin – it was all that early group, with Johnny Allen. I think it was probably Johnny Allen who broke the ice, because I had met him at Cassien, and he said, "Oh yeah, I remember you from Cassien." Then we all went down and celebrated together down the pub; it was a good little scene to be in, and I was enjoying it there. I was gutted I lost that fish, on the second weekend on there. I'd had a chance and they all said, "Well that'll be your chance for the year," and I thought, yeah right, I'll be having a few more of them, but of course, they were dead right. It was my only chance of the year and it's something that has happened to me a lot over the years when I look back at waters I've fished, especially English waters, and hard waters. I tend to go in full of confidence, and quite often

I get a take first or second night, or certainly in the first few nights, but a lot of them I have lost, and that was one of them at Fox Pool.

As the weeks went on, the takes weren't happening. Other people were catching the odd fish, and I was starting to lose confidence in what I was doing. I know Rob Maylin wrote about it in Fox Pool when he was fishing there before he caught the Parrot; you're winding yourself up about whether you're doing the right things. I read it again myself the other week, and I thought that's exactly what I was doing, but I didn't really know a way out if you know what I mean. I didn't know what the answer was, so I kept plodding away, and really, really struggling. The following year, well, I met Rob and the other guys of the Famous Five, and although I wasn't catching myself, they were fantastic times. I saw virtually all of the fish that year; Rob caught most of them, and I remember Clive Williams having a great year that year, catching Jack and a few of the others. It was the most disappointing time of my whole angling career I think, because the lake ended up being drained, all the fish were taken out, and I never did catch one there. I fished Fox Pool for two years, and I never caught one in that time. I really wanted to catch one too, so that was one of my real frustrating times. The same thing was happening at Johnson's; I was struggling there too, so I needed something that was going to get me out of that, if you know what I mean. I couldn't find an answer on either of those lakes, so the only thing I could do was go and fish another lake, and do something a little bit different for a while.

I still kept my Dartford Angling Club permit, but I hadn't fished any of their waters for years. It was about that time when the fishmeal boom was happening and Terry Dempsey and Tony Moore were the ones who brought it to Darenth. I was going up and seeing them, and even helping roll the boilies sometimes, because it was just good to see, and they were absolutely taking the Tip Lake apart. The fishmeals were a fantastic bait, and even better after a bait like the Richworths had been on there. It seemed like the Richworths would work for a year and then stop; the fish just didn't seem to want them too much any more, and it was almost like as soon as the fishmeals went in, it was everything they were looking for in a bait, and they loved it. They couldn't get enough of them; they were taking the Tip Lake apart on the Premier Baits with the Fish Feed Oil, and the fish were putting on weight. Well just down the road from Darenth was Sutton Lake, a very similar sort of lake, a shallow gravel pit, with loads of gravel bars in there. I knew the Richworths had been used on there for the last couple of years, but I knew too that no one had been using fishmeals on there, whereas Darenth was always a bit ahead in the bait stakes, because people from all

I arrived on December 28th just in time to see 'Nod' with Fox Pool's most famous resident, Jack, at just over 40lb.

Dave Whibley had got it right on Fox Pool and had a great season. Here he is with the lovely Big Scale at high-30's.

I took a break from Fox Pool to fish back at Sutton Lakes.

Sutton was a nice water to fish, and had not been done with the fishmeals yet, so I felt it was there for the taking.

I experimented with my own fishmeal mixes and came up with a winner!

around the country were fishing there. Sutton was still a local carp water, and so the people were slower to get onto things.

I thought to myself, well, if I can go to Sutton with the fishmeals, I reckon I'm going to catch a few there and get my confidence back. My confidence needed a boost, but I still had that stubborn streak in me, and I didn't want to use the Premier fishmeals; I wanted to make my own fishmeal. God knows why; it's daft really, but I've always had this stubborn streak, and I want to do things my own way, not someone else's way. So I was making all these fishmeal mixes, and most of them fell to bits, ending up in the bin, and then all of a sudden one day, I made this mix and it rolled nicely. It had loads of fishmeal in – more fishmeal than most other baits around at that time. I was using the Premier Fish Feed Oil but this mix was mainly capelin and sand eel meal. It isn't available now, but it was one of the main ingredients then, and it was a good one, along with sardine and anchovy, and a bit of Sluis and CLO, which was from a Dutch company, a bird food but it was a good one, a bit of casein, and bit of Codlavine, which was like a cod liver oil. I put it all together, it made a good bait, and the fish loved it.

So I went down to Sutton armed with my fishmeals and that first weekend, I caught one. I remember catching a 20lb linear, and you know, it was just a weekend session, but I caught one, and I was so pleased to catch a fish. It was like I was never going to catch one again on Fox Pool and Johnson's; they were too hard, and I'd gone down and caught a fish, and I thought brilliant, I'll have some more of that. The next weekend I went back and caught two or three, or it might even have been four, and the more I

Early fishmeal success at Sutton with a 25lb mirror.

put in of the fishmeal, the more the fish came. Some of the other guys were still on the Richworths, and they'd had had good years the year before, but they just stopped catching. As soon as the fish found the fishmeals, they wanted them and nothing else, and I sort of knew it was going to happen because I had seen it happen at Darenth, and the lakes were so similar, only just down the road. I thought well, it's there for the taking if you know what I mean, and as soon as they went in, I started catching. Over the next few weeks, I suppose I had about 15 or 20 fish, all good fish too. They were the same sort of strain as the Brooklands fish, the old Galician strain mirrors, with big blade-like scales. They were lovely fish, and quite old fish too, probably stocked in the 50's or 60's, but they were great, and they just loved these fishmeals.

It didn't seem to matter where I fished, if I could find little bits of gravel I would just bait up the spots and fish would come to it. There were a few other guys who started to come down – Paul Madden who had fished on Darenth, and a few other guys like Stevie Gee and Colin, and they all started to get on them as well. We were all catching fish and plenty of them, and 20's were about top of the range. I fished next to a guy called Sam one weekend, who now works for Martin Locke, and I caught a brace, one of which was 28lb 2oz. I remember that, because it was actually a lake record mirror, and I had them both in the net at the same time. I also had a few other 20's that weekend, and it was, I wouldn't say too easy, but it almost seemed like that. Wherever I was putting the baits, the fish were coming and picking them up, and other people were have a bit of a tough time. But it was just those fishmeal baits, because four or five of our little group who were using them, were all catching good fish, and it was just a really, really good little time.

It was all halted in the end, as we had a bit of a drought that year. It was quite low water, and I went down there and set up one day and the bailiff came round and he said, "You'll have to pack up; we've shut the lake," and that was it. I had to pack up and go home, and that was the end of my little stint, but it was a fantastic two or three months' fishing, and I had got myself back on track after all the tough times that I had had before. I had done something that I needed to do, and gone out and got a few fish under my belt.

I suppose it was a bit of a funny old time. I went back to Cassien that year, and of course, I was expecting Cassien to be quite easy. I had caught a 40lb'er and a 60lb'er in my first two trips, and on my third trip, I was looking through all the pictures of what people had caught, wondering which ones I'd catch this time, but I went back there and blanked. I went in the August, and it looked lovely, as good as ever, but I sat there for two weeks, and never saw a fish show. I moved all over the lake, and in the end I was moving every day, trying to find fish, but never did, and never caught a carp. All I caught was bream, and I came away from there and it was like a real reality check; they were normal carp after all. It wasn't this Promised Land where you just go and bag up with loads of big fish; it was carp fishing the same as everywhere else. Yes, they were naïve carp and you could catch them, but when they weren't having it, you weren't going to catch them, and it was a long way to go for a two-week blank, just to sit in the sunshine.

But there were other things going on at the time, and I also had my first trip to Holland. I had met two Dutch guys while we were down at Cassien on my second trip; they had come up and seen a couple of the fish we had caught. We got chatting and they did say that any time we wanted to come over to Holland, they could sort us out with something perhaps on the

Most of the Sutton carp were old, but they were real scaly stunners.

Three of the best guys I fished Sutton with (from left) Colin, Stevie Gee and their friend Andy with the result of their night's work.

I fished midweek nights and would often have a couple of 20's before packing up for work.

canals or something like that. I had never fished any of the canals, but one of the things Holland was really known for in those days was for 20lb commons, and you know, it doesn't seem possible now, but in those days we didn't catch 20lb commons. If you caught commons they were singles or doubles; there just weren't many 20lb commons about, and quite a few people actually went to Holland to get a 20lb common. Anyway, we went over, and I think it was in 1988. I went over with Mandy and Mick Daly who we had met on Darenth, and we fished on the Twente Canal, and I remember putting out all this maize. They said you've got to bait up with maize, and it was a bit of a slow start, which surprised me, because we could see these fish swimming up and down, and I thought as soon as we'd put a bait in the water we were going to catch them.

We literally had to cut our swims out of the reeds, as no one had fished

One more good mirror of 28lb-plus towards the end of my Sutton stint.

anywhere along this stretch of canal before. I thought it was going to be easy, but for the first 12 hours, we never had a bite, and I thought something is going on here. I thought they had stitched us up, put us in this stretch where no one ever catches anything, but then after about 12 hours, I caught one. It was only a little one, but I thought at least we've got one, and then all of a sudden we caught another one, and it just gradually built up, and soon we were catching loads. All these carp suddenly turned on to the maize that we were putting in, and we caught loads of them. I got my first 20lb common, it was 22lb, and you know, like I say, it was what I had gone there for. I don't know how many carp we caught, but it was a lot. It would normally be quiet during the nights, but then in the morning, they would start to feed, and that would carry on for most of the day.

You had to watch out for the barges and all that, because there were great big barges going up and down the canal, and if you didn't see them coming, you'd wake up to a screaming run thinking you'd got a fish, but you'd got a 20-ton barge on the other end, and that did happen a few times. But it was good, and I remember the last night, John, the Dutch guy who we had gone over with, had a 27lb or 28lb common, which sort of showed some of the potential of what was in there. It was still a very big fish, and I think it was the biggest common I had ever seen then, and to put it in perspective, Albert Romp had had a 34lb common out of Cassien, which was a lake record at the time. Big commons just weren't about then, so a 27-28lb'er was a big common, and it looked really nice, so we were quite impressed with all that, and quite enjoyed it.

But then it was back to the other lakes really, and a few things happened. I remember coming home and finding this letter from Leisure Sport; I opened it up, and it was something like, "We are sorry to inform you that you've broken this rule, and that rule, and you're banned from Leisure Sport for life." I thought, Jesus Christ, what have I done? I'm no angel and I've done a few things, but I haven't been caught for any of them, so I was gobsmacked to get this letter. So first thing, like you do, I went down to see the head bailiff, and he said "You need to speak to the regional coordinator." So I rang him up, and he said, "No, you need to speak to the head bailiff. In the end, I rang up Jack Ashford, and I said, "Look, I know I haven't broken these rules, so what's going on?" He said, "Well, it's down here that you have broken these rules," and I said, "Well, you just tell me when it was reported, and when it was meant to have happened, and I can tell you exactly where I was, and why it hasn't happened." Anyway, he said, "Well it doesn't matter – if we want to ban you, we can ban you." So I said, "Well is there nothing I can say to change your mind?" He said, "No, you're

Fishing Holland for the first time on the Twente Canal.

It was quiet and unpressured on the Twente Canal – we even had to cut our own swims out.

My first 20lb-plus common at 22lb – one of the things that I went to Holland for.

Back on the Railway and the key to success was getting a microwave to make some proper pop-ups!

Mick Daly and I with four Dutch carp. Once we started catching it became almost constant action.

My Dutch friend John with a high-20 from that first trip.

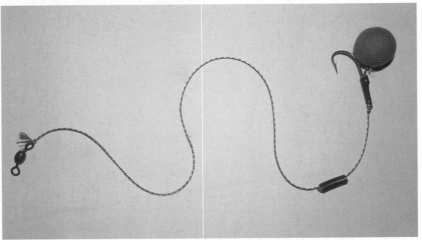

I was so confident in the rig and pop-ups that I knew I would catch!

Not a big'un but an important step in my fishing at the Railway.

banned" and that was it.

I was gobsmacked because I knew I hadn't really done anything to deserve getting banned. It was year later when I actually spoke to a few people who let on that they were old Darenth bailiffs, and they let on who was behind it all. I'm not going to go into the whys and wherefores, but it was a stitch-up. I knew the bloke who had put the spoke in for me, and it was nothing to do with any rule breaking. It's the old story; I was probably catching a few too many fish and upset a few too many people – it always happens. It was the first time, but it wasn't the last time. It was a shock though, because it was the first time it happened to me, and I wasn't expecting it. Looking back it was probably a good thing in a way, because it got me out fishing other waters. I probably would have gone back to Darenth and carried on fishing there when really I needed to get out and fish other waters. So that was the boot up the arse I needed.

The other water I had was Johnson's, so I carried on fishing there for a while, and to be honest, in the end I did get it together. The thing that changed all of my fortune around was getting a microwave. It sounds daft now, but I was always struggling with pop-ups before. I knew I needed pop-ups; I needed them on Fox Pool, and I needed them on Johnson's, but I didn't know how to make them. Again, there were no pop-up mixes out there; everyone made their own pop-up mixes. I remember Rob Maylin having them at Fox Pool, and I thought God, he's got some good pop-ups, but I had no idea how he used to make them. I didn't have a microwave, and I couldn't afford one, simple as that. By the time I had paid the rent on my house, and put bit of petrol in the car, I couldn't afford a microwave, so I just had to go without, but eventually I got myself a microwave and I made these blue cheese pop-ups. I went down Johnson's with Wadey, and that first weekend, I caught one straight away. It was only 9lb 15oz, but it was a very special carp for me, as I had been fishing the Railway for three years by then, and all I had caught were the two off the top, even though I tried and tried to catch one off the bottom. Bearing in mind it was getting on for winter; the start of November, I went down the next weekend and caught another one! So all of a sudden I knew what I needed to catch them, and I had finally done it; I had finally got there. The only problem with that was, by then it was winter and you know, Johnson's was hard enough in the summer. I had a few little dabbles in the winter, but people normally just pulled off.

I do remember the next time I went back was the start of the following season. I know I had been down to Brighton to see Pete Jones, and he had just made up these little pop-ups with Martin Locke's Esterblend 12 flavour,

Back on the Railway for the start of the season in the End of the Willows.

After losing the first three, I then landed these two commons at the same time.

We had a few sessions on Johnson's Road Lake. Wadey was the first to score with this nice mirror.

It wasn't easy, but I caught some decent commons from the Road Lake.

and I smelt them and I thought, God, that's just what I need for the Railway. I said, "Can you me make up a little batch of pop-ups while we're here?" I wasn't going to be able to do them back home, so we made up some there, and I took them down to Johnson's. On opening week, I hooked eight, landing five and losing three. The first three of them I lost because I was using these star point hooks. Before the start I said to Pete, "Look at these hooks, they're nice," and he said, "Don't use them. I know people who have been using those hooks, and they reckon they're rubbish; they keep losing fish on them." Anyway, I went with them, and I lost the first three I hooked, so I changed over to some Mustad O'Shaughnessy hooks, and the next five I landed. I didn't have any of the big ones; they were all 20's I think, with maybe a couple of double figure commons, but I remember the Leather got caught that week. There was one guy up in the corner, and it was the only fish he caught, but he had the Leather, which was the one I really wanted. I

A cracking Railway mirror that came during a hectic afternoon.

never got it, but I was so pleased to get those fish that I did catch after struggling for so long.

To be honest, that was the end of my fishing on Johnson's. I should have stayed on I suppose and tried for the Leather, but other things were happening. We had all fished on Johnson's during that time, and Rob Maylin had come down there with the other guys; Steve Alcott, Dave Whibley, Phil Harper, and they had all caught good fish, and by then had moved onto Harefield in the Colne Valley. I had stayed on to do the start on Johnson's, but once I had caught those fish, I thought well, that's it; I know I can catch them now. I almost I felt that I had overcome the barrier, and I wanted to come up to the Colne Valley and fish with Rob again, so that was the end of Johnson's.

Same time next afternoon and another fish! All of a sudden it was so easy.

Chapter 5
Harefield and Farlows

"It was another big gravel pit and to me that meant fishmeal"

Around 1990, the end of my Johnson's fishing, was also the start of my Colne Valley fishing. We had all done a fair bit of fishing together then, with Rob, and the other guys, and I remember him saying to me, "Come up to Farlows in the closed season. It's open in the closed season when everywhere else is shut, and you can go up there and have a good laugh. There's a bar there, and a few fish to be caught, and it's something to do in the closed season." So I thought yeah, that sounds alright. I remember going up there that first time in the closed season, and Rob told me where to go, he gave me the directions. I had pulled up in front of the restaurant, expecting it to be on a different part of the lake maybe, but there was this restaurant slap bang in the middle of the lake out on the point, and all the swims were just around the outside, and they were all the swims he was fishing! I thought Jesus Christ; he wasn't joking.

I set up there, and the bar was 10yds away, and I just laughed; I remember sitting there just laughing thinking, this is alright. My fishmeal bait was still working, so I took that up there, and I think I caught four or something that weekend. They weren't anything big, but they were four little Farlows carp, and it was good fun. I mean the fishing was really only just a minor part of the whole Farlows experience; it was just good fun, and there was no other way to describe it. It was fun fishing because if the weather was alright you would be in the bar playing pool, having a drink with the patio doors open, and listening out for a run. I'd never done that before when carp fishing; I was always sat in the bivvy or whatever. I know the first night we were in there, we were all sitting round playing cards, having a drink, when suddenly Travolta disappeared out of the window, and I thought, what's going on? He had had a run; he'd heard it and I hadn't, and he went out and had this fish. It was a bit mad to be honest, but it was good fun fishing, and we caught loads of fish and had a good time.

I remember at that time, I had split up with Mandy, and that was when I met Joan, because Joan was manager of the bar and restaurant at Farlows. We got on quite well; we always used to have a good chat, so I started seeing Joan, and started staying up there longer and longer I suppose, but I was enjoying the fishing. Anyway, I actually came up to try and fish Harefield, but for some reason John Stent wouldn't let me have a ticket for Harefield. He had the hump with me about seeing Joan, I think, and he wouldn't let me have a ticket, which I was gutted about because everyone was on there. But the thing was, everyone who fished Harefield was allowed to take one guest on per season or something, and as everyone was already on there, there were no other guests to take on there other than me, so everyone took me as a guest for one weekend. I just ended up fishing it, and it got to the stage where I was on there every weekend, and no one said anything.

It was another big gravel pit, and to me that meant fishmeal. I had seen them work at Darenth; I had caught loads of fish at Sutton on them, and I figured that Harefield was made for the fishmeals, now I know you went in with the pop-up approach, launching it out to the fish, and you were catching really well too, but I was convinced in my own mind that fishmeals were the way to go at Harefield. I know the first time I fished Harefield I fished up the Causeway and I lost one, just fishing out over the bars, at the range I could bait up. It was easy to fish long-range because you were always seeing fish jump at long range, but I wanted to fish where I could bait up, and I lost one the first weekend, so it gave me the confidence to go on with that.

The second weekend I was on there, I started off on the Causeway. I walked all the way around the lake and every swim was taken. It was so busy, as Harefield had become such a mega water in the early 90's. John Stent had some funny ideas, but he also had a lot of vision, and he was a good guy. He had a lot of ideas about what he wanted to do, and one of them was to create a water that could compete with Savay. Savay was far and away the biggest and best water in the Colne Valley, and John Stent wanted to create something that could compete with that. How he did that was to drain Rodney Meadow, take all the fish out of there, and put them into Harefield. Willow Pool was the other water he took fish from, which caused a lot of controversy at the time, because there were a lot of people fishing Rodney and Willow Pool. They were their local waters, and all of a sudden they were being drained and the fish were being taken to create this super lake up the road. I can understand how they felt, but the difference for me was that I was coming up just after all that had happened. The fish had already been put into Harefield, so there was this fantastic lake that we were able to go and fish, and it was a fantastic lake – unbelievable at that time.

I think the only thing that gutted John Stent all through those years was that he never actually got the biggest fish out of Rodney. There was a fish in there called Big Rod, which was a mid-30, a big fish at the time. He reckons he saw it get over the net when they were netting it, and there were all sorts of rumours about what happened to it after that, such as some of the old regulars had gone back down there, caught it and moved it. To be honest, I don't know what happened to it, but I never saw another picture of it to this day. But it was the big fish, and it would have been fantastic in Harefield for sure, because there were a lot of 30lb fish in there. I think the only one that didn't go into Harefield was the Pet, and that went into Farlows. There had been a big 30 in Farlows before, which had gone missing

Farlows Lake in Buckinghamshire was my first experience of the Colne Valley.

I just laughed when I arrived, as our swims were just a few feet from the bar!

First Farlows carp, one of four or five that first weekend on the fishmeals.

The Pet, the biggest carp in the lake at 31lb 8oz, and just one of 14 carp that week-end.

somewhere, so the Pet was now the biggest fish in Farlows, and all the rest went into Harefield. There were somewhere between 15-20 different 30lb fish in Harefield, which was fantastic at the time. Darenth probably held the most 30's at the time, and Fox Pool had quite a few in – probably six or eight over 30lb. Johnsons probably had less than that, four or five maybe, and then you had Harefield, which had 15-20 in, and although it was a bigger water, if you could get on them, you had a real chance of a 30lb carp.

Anyway, the second weekend that I fished I walked all the way round

A memorable common, on the fishmeals again, and I think my first English common over 20lb.

and every swim was taken. I got round to the Pads where there was a swim empty, and I just beat this bloke to it. I was next door to Phil Harper using his ham pop-ups; I think he had got a job lot of ham flavour, and I think he's probably still using it now. Every time I saw him he was using ham pop-ups, but I put out my fishmeals, and next day about midday off it went. After a proper good old scrap, I landed a fish known as Small Pecs. I remember it, because it was the 17th different 30 out of Harefield that year, and it was only a month into the season – mid-July. That probably doesn't mean so much to people now, but in those days, that was mind-blowing. It was the first time that fish had been caught that year; it was my first Harefield carp, and it was a personal best English fish at 34lb 8oz, so I was well pleased with that one.

That was definitely going to be my fishing for that season. I would get there by hook or by crook, as long as I could avoid John Stent knowing I was there. I would sneak in and fish there, and it was amazing; everyone just kept it under their hat. They all knew I was fishing there, and it was great, with good people up there, and of course the Horse and Barge was just across the road. The Horse and Barge was famous already as the meeting place for the carp anglers in the Colne Valley, and it was brilliant. We had some great times over there – great evenings.

A couple of weeks later, I was back in the same swim and I had Small Pecs again. I didn't go up the pub that night for some reason; I just felt like I was going to catch one that evening, or I was a bit keen or something. It was about 10.30 and I had another run, and it was the same fish. It was a little bit bigger the second time at 35lb, and I had another one the same night, a 25lb mirror. I think I was four weekends into my Harefield fishing, and although it was the same fish twice, I'd caught a couple of 30's, and two personal bests, so it was going well – the old fishmeals were working, and life was good. Joan was finishing up the bar at night and coming down with pizzas and stuff after the Horse and Barge, so we had a good time up there. It was certainly a change to fish there; I mean my experience of fishing the Colne Valley had been Farlows where you were 10yds from the bar, or Harefield where you had the Horse and Barge just across the road, and it was that style of fishing. In the Darenth Valley that sort of thing didn't really go on; they were all super keenies, and you stayed on the lake and you fished. But in the Colne Valley, you didn't fish in the evenings; you reeled in and went over the pub. It was a different side to carp fishing for me, but at the same time, a really exciting part, because you didn't have to be sat on the bank all the time, twiddling your thumbs and waiting for something to happen. You had something to look forward to; you could reel in that evening, meet up with everyone, and have a good chat about what's happened and this that and the other. Then you'd get back, cast your rods out, and you might get a fish in the morning. You used to go home after the weekend and think well, that was alright. That was the carp fishing culture of the early 90's in the Colne Valley, and everyone did it, well, not everyone,

A change over to pop-ups brought a sharp rise in action.

A quick jaunt over to northern France brought me this hard-fighting mirror.

The reality of Chantecoq! It is a massive bit of water, and it meant a lot of rowing.

With a little help from my friends I finally made it to Harefield.

First Harefield carp – Small Pecs at 34lb 8oz.

Only four weekends into my Harefield campaign, and I banked Small Pecs again, at 35lb, along with a 25lb mirror.

Harefield wasn't the prettiest lake, but it held some fantastic carp.

Harefield was noted for its good commons.

but the vast majority of people did, and they were good times.

I suppose I should talk about the bit of French fishing that I still did. Harefield took up my English fishing, but when I had holidays, I still went away to France. One thing I had heard of was a little water in the South of France. Until this time all my foreign fishing had been on Cassien, with a couple of little trips to Holland to get the 20lb common. I remember being up at Farlows one time and Starman and Paul Boyd, who were always around Farlows, came in with these pictures of 30lb and 40lb mirrors, and they were lovely. They said "We've got a French mate who we've been out to see; he's got this little lake in the South of France, and we've caught all these fish, but we can't tell you where it is." I was looking at all these things thinking, 'Cor, I'll have some of that' and then the final comment was, "We'll show you the pictures but you aren't going to find out where it is." Oh shit! I could see where they were coming from, and I sort of forgot about it, but then a few weeks later I was talking to a carp angler in Uxbridge; I mentioned this lake, and he said "Oh yeah, I know that lake," and he blurted out the name. He said, "Yeah, it's that such-and-such lake down near Toulouse." So I went straight home, got the map out, looked for this lake, and sure enough I found it. I thought right, I know where it is, and I've got to go.

I know it wasn't a problem for me getting the time off work, but Joan had a bit of a problem, as we had just been to Cassien. I'd had another trip to Cassien and had a few there; a 30lb common or something like that. Anyway, somehow we wangled her another week off; I don't know whether she said she wasn't well or something. It was when Mickey Fry was running Farlows, and it was hard to put one over on him, but we managed to do it. I told Paul Boyd we were going down to this lake, because I thought if he finds out we've been, he isn't going to be happy, because it was all top secret. I went up to him in the bar and I said, "Look Paul, I know where the lake is now, and we're going to go down there, but I just wanted to tell you first." He just looked shocked, and asked, "How did you find out about it?" But what could he say? It was a public lake, so anyone could go and fish it. I could see he didn't like it, but he agreed anyway.

So we went down to this lake, and it was different to the other lakes I had fished. It was a man made lake, and had a little beach on one end. In fact we called it the Secret Beach Lake, just to keep it quiet. I remember it rained the whole week; it was horrible weather, and it wasn't that easy. With a boat you could more or less fish the whole lake from wherever you were on the bank. We tried a couple of swims, and I remember seeing these fish jumping at the other end, so we moved over. We actually set up on the little beach, and I caught three fish that first night once I got on them – two 30's and a 40, which were still mega fish in those days. There was no one else on the lake at all, and I caught another 30 the next day. Then loads of people turned up; I remember a couple of French guys setting up on the other bank, and then three blokes walked down to me on my bank. I thought I recognised them, and it was Roger Smith, Roger and Kerry Barringer. They had met this French guy at Cassien who said, "I know of this little lake we can go to," so they turned up on this lake and hey presto, we were all there together.

Even in those days it was a very small world, carp fishing. You could go a thousand miles from home and then see someone who lives just round the corner and things like that. It was tough after that, because there were so many people on there. One thing I remember is that all the fish moved out from the beach where I was fishing, and as soon as everyone set up, it all went quiet. There was one little bit in the middle where no one was fishing, and I thought if I were a carp, that's where I would be, sitting out there in the middle. So I blew my boat up, took a little bit of bait out there, and dropped it. They were the same sort of big baits I was using at Cassien; the big rock hard baits with just a few freebies around, and the next morning it went off with a 50lb'er on the end. 50lb 8oz it was; a nice dark mirror with little starburst scales on it. It was a brilliant trip; I just sneaked down there, and we were fishing for six days, or something like that. It was the first other water I had fished in France other than Cassien, so that was nice to do.

We're up to 1994 now, and the only other French water I went to that year was Chantecoq with Pete Jones. We fancied venturing out a little bit more; Cassien was always a long drive, I never minded driving down there, but the other big waters around Paris were starting to get known – the Orient and Chantecoq – so we decided to go out there. It was easy fishing to be honest, and the only difficult thing at Chantecoq was the conditions, which I don't think Pete was quite ready for at the time. I suppose neither of us were really. We drove down to the famous Church Swim at Chantecoq, just as two Dutch guys had packed up and gone home, so we were lucky. We got in that swim, which was probably the best-known swim in Europe, and we were lucky with the weather as well, as it had been red hot all week, and everyone around was catching nothing. This guy came round to us, and he said, "I've been here all week, and haven't had a bite yet," and I thought Christ, I thought it was going to be easier than that

But that night, the rain clouds moved in and it started raining, the wind got up, and as it happened we just turned up on the right day. The guy who hadn't caught anything, and whose last night it was, came round with three

A cracking Harefield linear during my first year.

One of the named fish, Stripes, which fought incredibly hard.

I caught plenty of carp from the small island, although no real monsters.

Early 1990's at Cassien just after a big fire had swept through the region. This was my first trip with Joan, and we fished on the island in the centre of the picture.

Joan with her first Cassien carp after quite a tussle.

Only three rods were allowed then at Cassien, and we always hired our boat from Chez Pierre's.

A lovely Cassien common, and my first over 30lb.

Shortly after Cassien we were off to the Secret Beach, a small water in France that wasn't easy, but once I was on them it started to happen big time!

sacks in the morning for us to photograph his fish. It all started happening; Pete had the first one I think, at 28lb, and I caught a couple of doubles. All of a sudden, it was just going off all the time, but it was very, very difficult fishing in other ways. There were so many snags out in Chantecoq; we were using tough English gear, with 15lb nylon and 4oz leads, that sort of thing, but looking back now, it just wasn't up to the job on that sort of water. But we did catch loads of fish, and I caught a 40lb'er. Pete definitely had the snaggier side of the swim, which was just the luck of the draw, because we didn't know before we set up, so he lost more than he landed, but he had 30's. We both had 30's, and I had the one 40.

I went back a few weeks later with Joan and fished Chantecoq again, but the other side of the lake, which was about five miles away – Chantecoq was huge. We caught even more; it was getting to the stage where you could catch as many fish as you wanted to catch. It was just a matter of how much you could put up with the rowing and walking through the mud. The water level went down so low, and literally it was knee-deep in mud. You couldn't set up on mud, so you had to set up on the hard ground behind, and you had to walk through the mud to the water's edge to land fish or put baits out, which could be like 60-70 yards away. It was exhausting work to actually get three or four rods out through all the mud, and then go out and catch three or four fish on those rods was hard work too. In the middle of the night, if all those three or four rods had gone off, you had to put them all out again if you wanted to carry on fishing, so that's what you did. It was really hard work, and then they'd all go off again, so after three or four nights, it was just too much

All I did in the end was put three or four rods out, and once they had gone off, I'd leave them in for the night and just be happy with those fish I'd had. It was the easiest fishing I had ever had in my life in terms of catching fish, but probably the hardest fishing I had ever had in terms of the work you had to put in to catch those fish. But it was good; I'd always wanted to catch some of those fish because I had seen the pictures of them, and they were nice looking carp.

One thing I definitely noticed with those carp, because they were very naïve, was that the bigger bait you used, the bigger fish you caught. It's an old wives' tale; you know, big baits for big fish, but I took some of these donkey chokers of 50-60mm with me, and they looked ridiculous they really did. I always put one rod out with one on, and literally every night the biggest fish would come on one of those big baits. I suppose the little fish just whooshed in and fed on everything else and the big baits were just left for the big fish; it's amazing how it works. At the time I was using Carp

Company stuff by then, the Milk Mix and the Nut Mix, making these great big things. I went to a show with them just afterwards; I forget where it was, down in Essex, or it might have even been Woking, and I did a little talk on Chantecoq. I said, "I've brought along some of these baits just to show you what I was catching on – you can have a look at them in the break." I wish I had never bothered, because they all just laughed at them. They had only fished in England where 14-15mm boilies were the norm, and an 18mm boilie was a big'un, so they were looking at these 50-60mm boilies and they didn't think I was serious; they were all just taking the piss really. I was wishing I had never brought them, but they definitely did work. Every single night the big bait did catch the biggest fish that night, and I'm talking about the big fish – upper-30's to low-40's.

It was mad fishing. I have never been back there since in all these years, and it was 14 years ago now. I had my fill of action from there, and it was good, but there was no challenge. I have always liked some sort of challenge in my carp fishing; it's always nice catching carp, but when they come too easily, the novelty wears off in no time. It was too much for me; I didn't want to catch that many carp. I wanted to catch less fish that meant more, if you know what I mean. So yeah that was it, and I never went back to Chantecoq after that.

I came back to England and I started fishing a couple of the lakes around Woking because I knew the guys at the Carp Company, and they said, "Why don't you come down and fish the lakes at Woking?" Langmans, I think was the name, run by Ron Buss, so I went down, and they were lovely waters, and a good bunch of people. Langmans was the one with the big fish in, so I wanted to have a little go there, but it had a reputation for being quite hard. I thought the old fishmeal bait would work down there. I set up one the evening, and the following morning there were a few of the lads talking down the bank, and one of them came up who was a bailiff. As I showed him my ticket, I had a bite; a few bleeps. I saw the line cutting through the water, and he said, "Oh that won't be a bite; it's just a liner," but it wasn't, and there was one on the end, but after about 30 seconds it fell off. Going back to what I said before, I quite often would get a take quickly on a water, but I don't always land them, which is a real pain. Again it happened there, and it was a hard water, but they liked the fishmeals.

I kept fishing there right to the end of the season really, and I did catch a few fish. I gave up with the fishmeals in the end, and went onto the pop-ups as winter moved on, and they seemed to be a bit better if anything. I never caught anything big out of there, but I caught some lovely fish. One that I remember sorting the picture out of the other day was this fully scaled

About to return a 'Secret Beach' 40; it was a magic trip.

I saved the best until last with this 50lb 8oz mirror.

Set up in the famous Church Swim at Chantecoq with Pete Jones.

Chantecoq was big, but it was also full of carp that weren't too hard to catch.

Chantecoq was very hard work in the conditions, but the carp were lovely.

I had my first winter trip to Cassien in 1994.

I was well pleased to land this 47lb 4oz Cassien mirror on a chilly January morning.

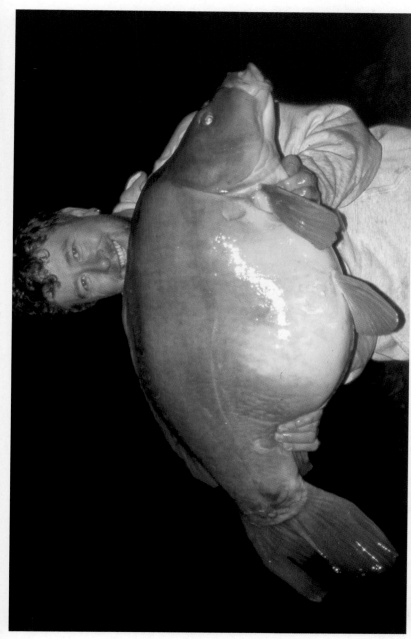

I was back at Cassien for another winter session in 1995 and ended up with another good fish of 47lb 12oz.

mirror that I caught, called the Armadillo. I remember that because they came round and said it hadn't been caught for two years or something, and it was a lovely fish – not massive, but I was well pleased with that one. I enjoyed my time down there; I didn't fish it much, but it was a lake that enjoyed fishing, and I met a few nice people on there. But it was never a lake I was going to carry on fishing; it was nice and there were some nice fish, but there wasn't anything really to keep me going back for more.

I fished the waters down at Woking a few times, and caught a few including this fully-scaled mirror.

Chapter 6
Summerleaze — A New Challenge

"We walked round Summerleaze that first time, and you could see that no one had fished it for at least two or three years, probably longer"

I was looking for a new challenge if anything, as I hadn't really got my teeth into an English water for a while. Harefield was probably the last water that I had committed a bit of time to, because there was something there that I really wanted to catch – lots of 30's. I was looking for a new water, and one came along that I had heard about before, called Summerleaze Lake. About the time I was starting to fish Harefield, a guy who fished Summerleaze Lake, Matt, had been fishing there for a few years, and he caught a 40 too. He said, "Why don't you come up and have a go at Summerleaze?" Well at the time, Harefield was just starting to happen, so I didn't want to go anywhere else. I just forgot all about it really, and it seemed like everyone did too. Hardly anyone knew of Summerleaze before then anyway, but there were some good fish in there. It had just been totally overlooked by people other than Matt, and he just happened to be down at Farlows a lot of the time.

I suppose it was during the closed season that year, or the early summer, there were a few of the guys down there, and all of a sudden we got the idea to have a go at Summerleaze. They were thinking about starting a syndicate on there, and I think before then you literally just had to go into the tackle shop and buy a ticket over the counter, which was probably why no one bothered; it was all too easy. All of a sudden when it was a syndicate, people thought it must be better. I think there was going to be a syndicate of 20 people on there; Matt and Paul Boyd were already on there from before, and you know, the rest of us were all basically new. Actually even Matt and Paul Boyd hadn't fished it for a few years themselves. Ian Russell, who was already on there, suggested getting a ticket, so we went up and saw it. The guy who owned the trout lake next door to Summerleaze had control of everything, so we went and got the tickets from him.

We walked round Summerleaze that first time, and you could see no one had fished there for at least two or three years, probably longer, because all the grass around it was more than knee deep, and there were no pathways through it to the bankside. There was a track around the outside where people used to go and feed horses on the other side, but you could see n one had even been to the edge of the lake; there were no paths. As soon as we walked through, there was a pathway through that stayed there forever, so definitely no one had been there before. All we knew was that these fish had been in there from years before, but there were rumours of a fish kill, so we didn't know what was going to be in there and what wasn't. For all we knew there might have been nothing in there. We started fishing it around March, and there was no sign of any carp whatsoever. I'm trying to think when it was, but I know the first bite I had was a tench, and it caused quite a bit of excitement because it was the first bite we'd had. We still hadn't seen any sign of carp or anything else, but I got this bite, so at least there was something alive in there. A few weeks later, just as spring was coming along, one of the guys called me, I forget who it was, and said "I'm fishing down one end and there are all these carp jumping out in front of me." So I thought, Christ, they are still in there, thank God for that.

Over the next few weeks, as the weather started to warm up, we started to see all these carp. There weren't many in there; I think the lake was around 60 acres, although it didn't look quite that big to me. There were a couple of other pits that were actually joined up to it through channels, so it was a fair bit of water. We started seeing these fish down in one bay, which was called No Carp Bay. Normally on lakes, No Carp Bay is where all the carp are, and it was no exception here. I mean it was good to be seeing these fish for a start; one because we knew there were carp in there, and two, because if they were the old carp then they were good fish a lot of these fish.

I'll always remember stories that Matt was telling us, because he had caught the 40, and that was the biggest known carp that had been caught in there. He was telling about this big fish in there, the big sandy mirror. He reckoned he was up a tree one day, and he was looking down and the 40 came in and was feeding underneath him. He had already caught it so he knew the fish, and then this other fish came in that was at least 10lb bigger, and he literally fell out of the tree he was so shocked, but that was all we ever knew about it. You always hear rumours about big fish, and you think to yourself well, sounds great, but who knows whether it's true or not? We all like to think it's true.

Well, one day we looked in this bay and there was the 40 and a couple of the others, and there was this sandy mirror. It sat there for best part of two hours I suppose, so I had a good look at it. We knew all the other fish alongside it, and it was definitely 50lb, and God, the excitement between us all. There were upper 30's, up to mid-40 possibly, and this other great big thing that had never been caught. To be honest, to this day I still don't think it has ever been caught; I don't know anyone who has ever caught it. I don't know how old it is or what it eats; its just one of those fish, but it's in there, or it certainly was. It gave us the buzz to go and concentrate on Summerleaze.

We were all more or less Carp Company boys at the time, and they did a very good fishmeal at the time, so we all went in with that. We mixed the fishmeal and a bit of salmon oil, and we all fished it. You could only fish one end of Summerleaze, as the other end was out of bounds. They were still working it, but luckily, the end we were seeing all these fish was the bit you could fish. I think Ian Russell was the first one to get a fish; he caught a 24lb mirror, and that was the start of it. We knew that all of a sudden this was the window of opportunity to catch the Summerleaze carp. There was one swim that I seemed to fish all the time more than the others, called Second Point or the Willows. I went in there, and there was no one normally fishing to the right and this guy Colin 'Gaylord' Nash used to fish further round, right up the end of the bank with his mate. Well his mate went on holiday, and he didn't want to be left up there on his own. I was down for a two-week session or something like that, and the next thing he was setting up in the swim about 10yds to my right and I thought, oh shit. I mean there was someone to my left, and he was where I had just marked out to fish. The area was really in front of him, so I was going to have to move over a bit. He was a nice guy, don't get me wrong, but I was gutted to seen him going in there; I couldn't believe it, but there we go.

Over the next few days it started to fish, and I caught my first Summerleaze carp, a 27lb'er. They were fantastic looking mirrors, like the old Leney strain, but oh, I was gutted. I missed out on a good opportunity really because to my left, Ian Russell had the Fully Scaled at 37lb something,

After a slow start, the fish eventually came out of hiding.

First Summerleaze carp on the Carp Company fishmeals at close range.

Colin 'Gaylord' Nash moved in next to me and caught the Summerleaze 40.

The Summerleaze 'Runt'. A friendly carp that I had a couple of times.

and Colin to my right caught the two biggest fish in the lake, a 44lb'er and the second biggest one, which was normally a 40, at 39lb the same day, and it was from the spot I was going to be fishing if he hadn't moved in. It's all ifs and buts; there's no saying I would have caught if I had been there, but you know, that was the chance if you know what I mean, and I felt like I had missed out, so I was a bit gutted. I did catch another fish that week, another 20lb'er, so we got in amongst them. I think between us we had six fish over that two-week period. We thought we were going to catch loads because we were seeing them all the time at that end, but really all they were there for was spawning. It was that that little period of pre-spawning, you know, and after that the fish started to drift away a bit.

We still caught the odd few here and there, but I do remember the weed was really, really bad that year. To start with, in April, May, June, it was alright, but then all of a sudden when the weed came up, since it was quite a shallow lake anyway, it was like a field out there; it was impossible to fish. The trouble was I was only a member of two lakes: Summerleaze, and another Colne Valley water just down the road, which has no publicity, so I can't really name it, but it was just down the road. All the others had other lakes; they had Silvermere and a few other waters, and they all said, "Oh we're going off to fish them now." I said, "Alright, see you later then." There was no sort of, "Do you want to come with us?" They just went.

I went and fished this other Colne Valley pit for a while, and it was another headbanger to be honest. It was a hard pit, but I went down there for a week, and the first week I was on there, I fished six days and never saw a sign of a fish. I was casting out, and it just seemed like I was wasting my time. Then on the Saturday, which was my last but one day of the session, they got a speedboat out – they used to do speedboat racing on there. As this speedboat reached the middle area, further out than I could cast, right out in the middle of the lake, these carp would jump. Every time it did it, out would come these carp, and I thought Christ, that's where they are but wondered how I was to reach them. The left hand bank to me was out of bounds, but I thought I know, I'll just cast onto the bank. It was all bare banks, so I could just go round, pick up the rigs, and walk them right along to where I had seen these fish jump, and just throw the rigs out and hope for the best.

The next morning, I had a 20lb 15oz common, and I just thought, oh well, it's a fish. I remember one of the bailiffs coming round, and he said to me, "That's the biggest common ever caught out of here; there's never been a 20lb common out of here before." He didn't like it at all, and they were a bit funny, some of the guys on there. There were some good guys and I got to know them all in the end, but it was their lake. Anyway, that was my first fish out of there.

I fished a few more sessions and nothing was really happening. It got to about September time and I thought, I don't know, I'll go back and have a look at Summerleaze. So I went back down there, and no one had been there since we had pulled off. I looked out and there was this clear channel in the weed. There was a lot of weed still there, but it was a slightly deeper little channel where all the weed had gone, and I thought, I don't know, that looks alright; it's fishable. So I put a bit of bait out, cleared some weed in the edge, and I thought, right, next weekend I'm fishing there.

I went back down the following weekend, and caught about half a dozen tench and a 21lb mirror. Again it wasn't a big fish, but it was a Summerleaze carp, and when there were only 17 carp in 60 acres, every one was quite special. It was one we didn't know; a lovely little fully scaled mirror; it was a beautiful fish. I thought, this is fantastic, you know what I mean; no one else knows I'm here. They've all gone off to fish other lakes, and I'm here on my own, and the fish were having it. So I thought well, fair enough, I'm not going to say too much. I put some bait in and came back the next weekend and caught another one. I thought if I can keep this going, I'm going have quite a decent result. That was five carp by then, all 20's. I'd had none of the big ones, but it was more than anyone else had caught.

Just before I packed up that weekend, I saw a little white van come in, and I knew whose it was. I thought, oh shit, I've been sussed. I'm not going to say who it was, but he came round and had a right old whinge because I hadn't phoned him up and told him I was down there catching these fish. Never mind that they had all gone off to fish their own water. The unhooking mat was still wet unfortunately. So that was the end of Summerleaze for that year. They all carried on fishing, but I think there was only one more fish caught that year. So that was it for that season.

The following summer, I went back with Pete Jones. Pete had got a ticket by then, and we were the only two on there. It was early in the year, with nothing much happening, and we saw the syndicate leader. He only lived across the road, which was why he was the syndicate leader I think, because he could keep an eye on it. He came through the gate with one of his mates and a boat, and I though, oh right, I didn't know anything about this, because they had actually stopped us using boats on there. It was a funny old syndicate right from the start; everyone was at each other's throats. Someone had taken a bait round the corner of an island with a boat, so instead of just having a word with him, saying, "Look you can't do that," they banned boats. You couldn't take a bait out with a boat, which was daft on a 60-acre lake, full of weed. There were rules where you didn't need rules – it was a 20-man syndicate, and we all knew each other.

But then we saw them turning up with this boat and thought, oh right. So we went round to see them and said, "Alright, how are you doing?" He went white because he didn't think anyone was on there, and we said, "What are you doing?" It didn't bother us too much, but he said, "Well look, keep it to yourselves, but I've been round to the boat club." There was a boat club who had control of the lake, and he said, "I've had a word with the main man in there about fishing off one of the islands down the other end," which obviously gave access to a lot of the areas that we couldn't normally fish. He said, "As long as there are only one or two people on the island, I can't see a problem with it," the old commodore or whatever he was. So the syndicate leader said to me, "It's me that's gone and sorted all this out, so do you mind keeping it quiet and just letting me and my mate have a few weekends first, because we've done all the hard work?" Pete and I said, "Fine, no problem, good on you for sorting it out. Go out there and have a go, and we'll have a go in a few weeks' time," which we did.

So they had their bit of fun, and then we came down with our boats and went out on the island. In the meantime, the same guy who had caught me fishing the year before came down in his little white van, saw our cars in the car park, and couldn't see us. Eventually, knowing we were there somewhere, he got out in his boat with one of the other guys, came out and found us on the island, and went into one, "What you doing out here, you're risking all out tickets, you can't fish out here, blah, blah, blah." We said, "Hold on, we've got something to tell you; we've got permission to fish off the islands. The syndicate leader sorted it all out for us, and all he asked was that we kept it quiet for a while, and it was up to him to tell all of the syndicate that boats were allowed." I can understand how he felt, but we had caught him on the hop a bit, so he went straight round to the syndicate leader's house and demanded that something should be done, and there should be a meeting about it. We were all asked to pack up and leave the island that day until they could have a meeting.

Well they had the meeting in our absence, and Pete and I got banned. It was a funny old syndicate, and it could be a bit like a witch-hunt. They'd ban anyone who wasn't there at the time I think, but we didn't really do anything wrong. We had permission to be on the island, all we hadn't done was tell everyone else that it was allowed, and that was only because we'd been asked not to. But the end result of the meeting was that we got banned from Summerleaze, so that was the end of my fishing there. It was a strange old sequence of events.

Everyone left because of the weed, but I went back and banked a couple including this little beauty!

Obviously I was gutted to be banned again, and it sounds like I'm always pleading innocent when getting banned from these places. But so far really, I still hadn't done anything wrong in my own eyes, but what can you do? These things happen in fishing.

I was still left with the other Colne Valley water to fish. I hadn't been banned from that one yet, and there was some lovely carp in that lake; some proper old Leney carp that I really wanted to catch. This particular lake used to be a lot bigger; it had been land filled, and they had lost a fair few of the old stock. But a lot of them were still in there, and among them were some big 30's, proper old scaly things, linears and all that; they were fantastic fish, so I decided to concentrate on that a bit more. I had that and my foreign fishing, so I had another trip to Cassien that winter.

Chapter 7
The Hutchy Years
— A Mixed Bag

*"Cassien, an English forty, Raduta, Africa
and a return to the Colne Valley"*

That really put my spirits up after getting banned from the other lake. I just felt like getting away from everything, and just going on waters where you didn't see anyone and no one bothered you. Cassien was perfect for that, and I had a great winter that year. What I remember that winter for was that it was the first time I'd done a long session in one swim. We literally sat for a month in one swim up the North Arm on the Second Point, and never moved; we just sat there through the whole lot.

It was good for a number of reasons, one of them being that I caught more fish than I'd caught on any of my other winter sessions. I started doing winter sessions in 1994 because they allowed night fishing on Cassien for the first time in the summer, whereas it never used to be allowed, so all of a sudden it was getting full up with people. The way to avoid them was do the winter trips, which at that time, hardly anyone was doing – Cassien was somewhere you went in the summer, but in the winter it was lovely.

We fished out from one of these points for a month and caught some lovely fish. I remember catching a 45lb mirror on January 1st, a New Year's Day fish, which was lovely, and also catching one in the snow. You always think of Cassien as being sunny and warm and all that, but we had one week during that session where it was dropping down to -10 at night. There was thick snow, which stayed for a week, and the action did slow up, but I managed to catch one before the snow went, which was a lovely fish to catch, and the first time I'd ever caught one in snow.

So all in all, it was a great trip and it cleared my mind. I forgot all about that was going on at home and all that, but then there was still the Colne Valley fish to have a go for when I got back. So as soon as spring started, I was back on there, and I did a few sessions in various swims around the lake. I remember doing one when it was bitterly cold; I'd baited up this little clear channel in the weed, put loads of fishmeal out, about 300 baits, and then fished a white pop-up over the top. I caught a mirror of about 21lb, and it was a time when any fish out of there was quite special really. You only ever really expected to catch two or three in a year out of there, so any fish was a good fish.

I also caught one by slinging a pop-up to a jumping fish in the middle, but other than that it was pretty quiet. It was about July time when I was walking around the lake, and I came to one corner and there were a few fish there. I hadn't seen anything anywhere else, so I thought it's got to be the place to be – at least I'm seeing fish. So I moved all my gear around to that corner, and I hadn't caught anything by the following morning, but I did see one of the quite big fish that hadn't been caught for about six or seven years. There were a lot of fish in there that hadn't been caught for years, and I remember looking at this big old grey one and thinking that there was a good chance of having something. So I sat there and fish drifted in and out, and in the afternoon the sun got up a bit. They were cruising round on the top, so I put a few mixers out and these fish started coming up and having the mixers.

I was scrambling around trying to set up a floater rod and firing out mixers, and these fish were still having them. There was one rod that I had left out, which was just cast into the weed. I'd been round and had a look at it, and the bait was actually resting just on top of the weed. I wasn't that confident in it, but that one went off. I was more excited about the floater fishing; I wanted to get the floater rod out. I thought it was bound to be a little fish or something, and I just wanted to get it in and out of the way. It charged through a few weedbeds, and gradually I pulled it in through all the weed. As it got closer I saw this line of scales, and I thought it was one of those 30lb linears or something, because there were a couple in there of around 30lb. As I got it in the net I looked down, and I though Jesus Christ, it's the big one. There was one in there, a double linear, and it was the biggest of the lot, which had been 38lb or 39lb, something like that. I couldn't believe it; I put it up on the scales and it was 40lb 6oz. I thought, I'm the only one here, and no one's going to believe me. I was wondering whom I could call, as Joan was up in Newcastle visiting relatives, so there was no chance getting her down. So I phoned one of my mates at work, who was plastering a ceiling or something. He said, "I'm plastering a ceiling, what do you want?" I said, "I just had the linear and it's over 40lb – any chance of coming down?" He literally he just dropped everything and came down, and so did a couple of the other guys, so there were about half a dozen of us there.

So we weighed it properly, putting it up on the tripod and it was 40lb 6oz, my first English 40, and a lake record as well. I was over the moon with that fish, because everyone wants their first 20 or their first 30 or their first 40 to be a really special one, and I don't think that there could have been a better fish in the country at that time for me to catch as my first 40. Gardner used to run a competition, Classic Carp of the Year; they used to have a monthly winner and a yearly winner, and that fish actually won it that year because it was so beautiful, which was just the icing on the cake really. We're talking about 11 years ago now, and that fish is long gone now. Unfortunately it died about five years ago now; they don't last forever, but it was a very, very special fish.

A lot of things started to happen for me during that time really. I'd always gone away fishing different waters, but it started to open up and

A cracking south arm mirror of mid-40's that came when the place was almost deserted.

Preparing the rigs for the night ahead at Cassien.

A Cassien summer common when I moved over to the dark side.

Big summer carp weren't easy to come by at Cassien, so this 43lb mirror was more than welcome.

A glorious winter's day in the north arm of Cassien.

A New Year's Day mirror of 45lb 2oz to get 1997 started in style.

It isn't always warm at Cassien; we had temperatures down to minus ten and a fair bit of snow, but I still managed to catch one or two.

All smiles as the needle goes past 40lb for the first time in England.

I always wanted my first English 40 to be special, but I don't think that it could have been any better than this one!

Doing a bit of pioneering in Portugal.

A Portuguese carp from a totally virgin water.

Lake Raduta – a new challenge and a water that really got me excited!

Perfect conditions on the wild and barren lake.

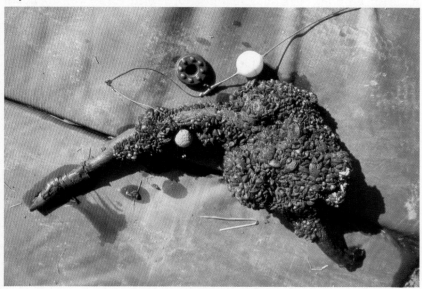

The snags were like nothing I'd experienced before.

spread out a lot more from 1998 onwards. I suppose one of the main things that happened this year was Fishabil and the World Carp Cup, which I fished with Tim Paisley. That was 2000, and only the second World Carp Cup, so I'm jumping a couple of years ahead, but we ended up winning that. I have to say I'm not a fan of carp matches or competitions at all; I can take them or leave them, and to be honest most of the time I'd rather leave them. But I have to say, when you're competing, doing well and you've got a chance of winning, they're brilliant. I loved every minute of that World Cup, and from the first day right through to the last we were in the lead. The feeling of actually coming through and winning one of those competitions was amazing. There were something like 90,000 visitors to that competition over the five days. There were even families clapping us at 2am, which was mad. I remember we were both in bed asleep; it was pitch black, about 2am, and I got a run. I got up for it, and there was a family behind us clapping. They'd obviously been standing there in the night just waiting for something to happen, and we were in the bivvies snoring. The whole event was weird, and there are loads of stories, but it was great to win it.

In 1998, I'd spoken to Rod Hutchinson a couple of times at the shows, and then all of a sudden I had a phone call when he was starting up the dream team, asking, "Do you want to be a part of it?" I thought blimey, yeah, I mean all I'd done something like it before when I was with the Carp Company, just getting bits of bait, but I'd never been a paid consultant for any of them. So I jumped at that chance, because I liked the idea of working with Rod and using his baits, and I was getting a bit of money as well. You could hardly call it a wage, but it was a bit of paid carp fishing, and I was all in favour of that. So that lead to a few things.

Another thing in 1998 was the discovery of Lake Raduta in Romania, which was to have quite a big impact on me and my fishing. I had three trips that first year in 1998, and then another one in 1999 with Pete Jones when we caught loads of fish. Pete had never caught a 40 then, and I hadn't caught a 40lb common, and we both caught 40lb commons, and we had them on the bank at the same time, which was fantastic. Those Raduta commons were fantastic; I have never seen commons like them – they were just gorgeous. Raduta had just done the world record, which until then had been held by some French bloke who had just caught this carp out of a river in France and knocked it on the head. Then all of a sudden one had been caught out of Lake Raduta, which was obviously still in there, and we could go and fish for it. I'd never fished for a World Record before, so that was exciting.

There was just so much going on, and we went to Africa in that little period too. Now you know I thought going to France to do a bit of carp fishing was good, but then there was Romania, and then all of a sudden South Africa. We flew out there; it was something like a 12-hour flight, and it was fantastic. We went out in February, and we walked off the plane and it was blazing hot sunshine, their summer, so how good was that? It was a fantastic place, and there was this lake right in the middle of the African bush. We had a bush fire in the evening, and you could hear the lions roaring in the distance, and there were huge spiders and things crawling all round. But there were big carp in there as well, and I think we had three 50's that first trip; I had a 54lb mirror, which made another country I'd caught a 50 from. France was the only place I knew of previously, well, in Raduta there was a chance, although I hadn't caught one, but I'd gone to Africa and caught one.

Also I drove all the way down to Portugal with Pete Jones, and it took us 17 hours – a hell of a journey. We got the Portsmouth to Santander ferry, which was 36 hours, and then it was 17 hours driving down to the lake. Christ it killed me, as I did all the driving. It was hard work, and we didn't catch big fish. The exciting thing about it was that it real sort of pioneering. I mean, I remember pulling up at this great big lake, thousands of acres, and we didn't even know if there was a carp in there. It was just this big expanse of water that we'd seen on the map. We just set the rods up, put the bait out, and it was weird sitting there thinking there might not even be a carp in here. But literally about four hours later, off it went, and Pete had the first one. Then we caught quite a few, nothing big, but it was exciting though because we just didn't know what we were going to catch, and it also proved the point that carp will eat boilies straight away. There were always these theories that you had to introduce boilies over the years, and on some waters you do have to, but there they just ate them straight away. It was good fun.

The only English fishing I did in that little period was when I went up to Hutch's water, Woldview. I fished up there a couple of times, and I caught a few up there, but again nothing big. I remember seeing his big fish, Floppy Tail, which was the first fish I saw on the bank when a guy caught it next to me. I caught a few fish, but otherwise, the only local fishing I did was on Rodney Meadow, which by then had been restocked, and there were some nice fish in there up to probably mid-30's, and it was nice and local. It was literally only round the corner from me, so I had quite a few sessions on there, mainly on the old Monster Crab pop-ups. I was making the old Monster Crab pop-ups with Shellfish Sense Appeal, and what a combination that was; it was just catching fish everywhere.

I remember doing the start of the season down there one year. I'd gone into the car park for the draw, and there were about 12-15 of us. I try to pull

My first 40lb common came during my first really good Raduta session in May 1999.

Raduta could be hell to fish, but at times it was heaven too.

Pete absolutely loved Raduta for some reason…

A special moment with a big Raduta common of 53lb.

Glum got his own back with this 41lb 8oz common.

On our way to winning the 2000 World Carp Cup at Fishabil.

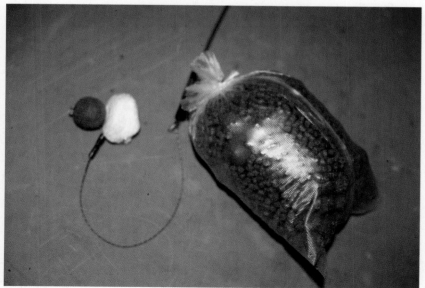

I must have tied up hundreds of these during the match.

I have to admit that this was quite a special moment.

The Hutchinson away team basking in the South African sunshine.

South Africa was about as exotic as it could get for a carp angler.

It took a while, but this South African mirror of 54lb was well worth waiting for.

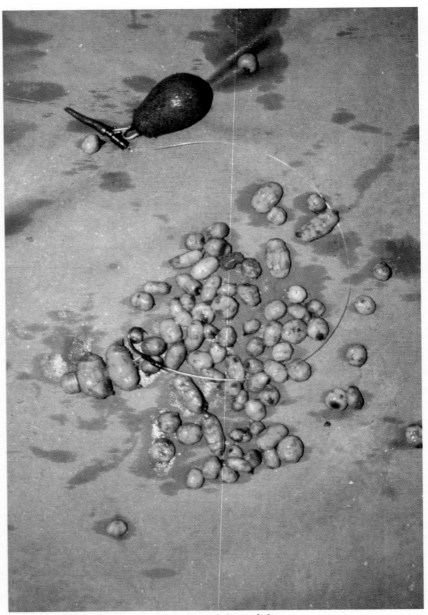

It had to be tiger nuts in Africa because of the catfish.

My fishing partner in Africa, Sandy Hough, with a good mirror.

Back at Cassien for the winter.

Getting our longest-ever session off to a great start with this 47lb 14oz lump.

A fantastic Cassien 50 that came when I thought feeding time was over.

the old stroke of folding your card in half to get it pulled out first, and got sussed out straight away. They pulled it out and they said, "You ain't gonna get away with that!" I thought that would be a new one on them, but it wasn't. I got this swim anyway around the middle of the lake where I'd caught a fish before. Ginger Steve was there, but he wasn't fishing; he was just down there to see what was going on. I told him the swim I'd got, and I said, "I've caught fish from there before," and he said, "Well, you might catch fish from there, but everyone else on the lake is gonna catch more than you – I guarantee it." I think I had 14 fish over the next three or four days, and there were only about 20 fish out. I caught them all on these little Monster Crab pop-ups. All I was doing was just casting onto the bars; there were two main bars running up the lake in front of me, and I was just casting the little pop-ups on top of the bars. The fish were cruising up and down the bars and just picking them up; it was easy peasy. So that was my little bit of fishing on Rodney Meadow; it didn't last long but I had a good bit of fun on there.

I suppose after that Colnbrook West was the next water I got involved with a little bit, which was another one of the Boyer Leisure waters. They've got quite a few nice little waters all dotted around the Colne Valley, and most of them have got some sort of decent fishing on them. There are no record breakers, but there were a few nice fish here and there, and Colnbrook West had this one that was a mid-30. This was when a mid-30 was still a big fish, and it was only four acres, so I thought, that's somewhere else to have a little go at that's not too far away. I thought it would be a nice fish if I could catch it, and it sounded like it got caught a few times, so it shouldn't be too hard, and I set about having a go for it.

I really enjoyed fishing there; there were loads of fish in there, and I've never seen carp that were so active. You could always find carp in there, and whether they were cruising about, jumping or bubbling, there was always something to get your interest going. The people on there were great as well; here were no names on there or anything like that, but everyone always seemed to get on alright, so it was good in that way. I suppose this fish did get caught a few times, but it always seemed to be after I'd gone home, or before I got there. I'd get down there at the weekend and I'd hear, "Oh Warty was out on Thursday." So I thought right, I've got to get down there and do a week's session when no one is there. So I got down with Joan actually, and I was fishing this swim that had a plateau out in front. I had a couple of pop-ups, Scopex and Esterfruit, out on this plateau. There wasn't much about, but I saw this fish right over in the far corner, the first one of the morning up on top with its back out, and it was like, oh, there's one over there in the corner.

Over about a 20-minute period, this fish cruised up and down, zigzagged across the lake, and gradually got closer and closer to where we were. Eventually it came up to the plateau, and just when it was where my baits were, just over them, it disappeared. I looked at the rods, and one of them went off. It got weeded straight away, but I played this ball of weed in, and hey presto, it was Warty in there. I was a bit unlucky with the weight I suppose, as it had actually been nearly 45lb at the start of the season, and when I had it, it was 36lb, all spawned out. So I'd caught the fish I was after, but I thought to myself, I'll have to go back and try and get it at 40, because it was over 40. So I did make my mind up to keep having a go back there if I could, and I did, but I was a bit unlucky at different times.

One session I was down there for five days again, midweek, and I had it all to myself, and was catching plenty of fish. I think I'd caught 20 fish or something in the first three days from this one little area; they were really having it and I thought, I'm gonna get Warty here, no problem. Anyway, this guy came down, Colin Webb, who had caught Warty about ten times; it was like his pet. Every time he came down it was like, "Oh, I've got Warty again." He said, "I'll go round up the back in the swim up there," so off he went. Well, ten minutes later he came back, and I thought he'd forgotten something, but he said, "You got any scales? I've got Warty." Apparently he had cast one rod out before he had even set up the second one, and it had gone off with Warty on the end. So that made 11 times that he'd caught it, and he had only been there a couple of minutes. So I went round, and it was 41lb 12oz and I thought, I was sure I was going to catch it.

So I thought to myself, right, the best chance I've got is to go back in the opening week of the season, the following season. It opened on May 1st, and I knew there was always a chance of that fish coming out in opening week. Generally it always got caught opening week, and I thought well, throughout the year there are probably 110-150 members or something who go down there, and you've got to compete with that lot through the year, but if you're there opening week and there are 12 or 15 people, you've got a one in 12 or 15 chance of catching it. I ended up getting the swim I wanted anyway, and it was a bit of a slow start, but I got this area of bait established out in the middle, the old Hutchy MC mix it was. I was fishing white pop-ups over the top again, and I caught quite a few fish. Then off it went again in the afternoon, and I knew it was Warty because of the weight of it. It took a long time before I even saw it, but I netted it, and it looked much bigger than before, and definitely over 40lb.

I put it on the scales, and it went 38lb – oh no! Normally I'm not one

Out in the boat with Joan playing a personal best mirror.

Back on home ground at Rodney Meadow.

A New Year's brace of Cassien carp.

Playing a fish hooked from the margins.

A nice Rodney Meadow mirror that fell for a Monster Crab pop-up.

The Monster Crab pop-ups just seemed to catch me fish wherever I took them.

"Everyone will catch more than you," said Ginger Steve.

Colnbrook West was a small water that held a big fish.

Pop-ups over fishmeals did the job and I caught fish every trip.

The winning combination for Colnbrook West – pop-ups.

Warty captured at last! But down in weight at 36lb.

A big storm sweeps across Lake Raduta

I normally adopted a pet for the session.

A classic Raduta common of high 40s from a freezing October session with Simon Crow.

Back to Colnbrook West for the start and Warty graced my net again at 38lb.

for recaptures, but I wanted to catch it at 40, but it was never gonna happen for me. It got caught about ten times that season, and that capture was the only capture under 40lb. Literally got two weeks later it came out at 40lb 8oz, and every capture for the rest of the season was over 40, but you know, you can't win them all, and you've just got to accept it. It's another fish that's gone now, old Warty, but it was a proper old character in the Colne Valley, a nice target fish to catch, even if I couldn't get it at the right weight.

I went back to Raduta with Glum. I was doing a bit of work with Glum, bless him; he died himself a couple of years ago now, and he was a good mate. He did me a lot of favours, so I took him out to Raduta. It was quite funny really, because we set up in this swim and I said, "What do you want to do for sides, toss a coin?" He said, "No you just have whatever side you want." So I said, "Alright, I know what side I want," which was the right hand side of the swim. I'd fished it before with Pete Jones, and we both caught fish, but there was this one spot that I thought, I know if I ever go back there, that's where I want to fish, so that's what we did.

I didn't catch loads of fish but over a three-day period I caught a 41 one day, a 45 the next day and then a 53lb common. They were all commons, and Glum's face was a picture every time; I mean, the words that were coming out of his mouth just got worse every time – it was so funny. I think the biggest he caught was about 16lb or something, bless him, but he got his own back on me. It was funny, but that was my first 50lb'er out of Raduta, which was my third country that I'd caught a 50 from, and a 50lb common too. I'd never caught one of those before, so that was a bit special in itself.

Cassien was again featuring heavily in the fishing I was doing. Again the rules had changed down there; they were always bringing rules in to try and stop carp anglers doing something or other. Cassien is a lovely place, and loads of tourists go down there during the day. Of course they get to come down to this nice little beach with their picnic hamper, and there's some smelly old carp angler bivvied up there, who's been there for about three weeks, and there are flies buzzing round the bivvy. So I suppose they thought, we can't really have that, so they stopped night fishing in the summer between June and September, and you could only fish during the day. Well of course the first thing everyone thought was, what's the point of driving all that way when you can't even bivvy up and stay on there at night? So everyone stopped going there, and I went down with Joan, and the place was empty.

The thing was, because there was no bait going in, the fish were looking for bait, and it was like a different lake to the Cassien that I'd known over the last few years. All of a sudden, instead of waiting a month for half a dozen fish, you could catch up to ten fish in a day, and they were everywhere. We would go in a different swim every day, and whatever swim we went into, there were fish there, and we were catching them – it was brilliant. We were the only ones there, and it was the nearest thing to going back to the old days when I first started fishing there. That was fantastic in itself, but probably the winter trip that year in 2002 was one of my most memorable.

It was the first time we'd fished in the South Arm; we always used to go up to the North Arm of the lake to fish in the winter. We went to the South Arm, again armed with the old MC Addicted baits, which I was full of confidence in. I knew they were going to work at Cassien in the winter, and you know, they did. I was catching fish from the start up to over 40lb, and I remember one rod going off; it was Joan's rod actually, but she didn't like going out at night. That rod had gone off twice, and I'd gone out like you do, just to get the fish so she didn't have to go out in the boat. The fish were 31lb and 39lb, I remember that, and then I had to go off to the shops, and so I said, "I'll only be an hour or so and I'll be back."

As I was coming back from the shop, I could see the same rod was wound in, so I knew Joan had caught one. I thought fair enough, and got back to the bank and she said, "Eee pet, I've had one. I don't know how big it is, so I've just left it in the landing net over the side of the boat." "Oh right," I said, and put the shopping in the bivvy. I looked at the fish, and thought, Christ, that's big, and it was 60lb 4oz, and I was blown away; I was so happy for her. There are quite a few people who have said to me that I must have been gutted, because if I'd stayed on an hour I would have had that fish. But no, I was over the moon for her, because you know, Joan loves Cassien as much as I do; she loves fishing as much as I do, and most times it's the old story that I do all the fishing while she's sitting there enjoying it if you like. But she likes to catch fish herself, and the thing was, I'd gone away and she'd done that all by herself. It had got snagged up, and she had to wait for it to get out the snags.

It's not even the first time she's done it; a couple of years earlier she had broken her leg while we were on Cassien. We had just moved into a new swim, and I had to pick her up in the boat and row her back to the swim, and she said, "I've hurt my leg, but we're not going home, we're staying here. I'll be alright." Well, about a week later we hadn't caught anything, and it was January 1st, and I had to go and get the new permits. I had to leave her, and went off to get the new permits. I came back an hour later and she was sitting in the edge of the lake. I could see her from about 200yds away,

Night fishing was banned in the summer at Cassien but it opened up a whole new world of possibilities.

A 44lb common caught during a hectic filming session.

Fishing days-only at Cassien was hard work – but worth it!

A 50lb 12oz Cassien chunk that came during the hottest part of the day.

Out in the boat again and I knew this was a good one.

Another winter's night draws in down in the south of France.

55lb of Cassien mirror – in fact this is now Cassien's largest carp.

A 51lb 12oz mirror that came from a reliable spot.

It was the first time we really targeted the south arm in the winter, and it turned out to be a good choice.

I came back from the shops and Joan had this in the net! 60lb 4oz of Cassien mirror!

It was a great winter session with plenty of good fish for me too, topped by this 51lb 12oz mirror.

and I thought, Jesus Christ, she's fallen over or something. Well I got back to the bank, and she was sitting there in the margins with a landing net and a rod, and she'd had a 41lb mirror. She had to shuffle around on her bum because she'd got a broken leg, but she caught this 41lb mirror, and again did it all on her own while I was away. How she did that I don't know, but this time she had gone one better with a 60lb'er. Fair play too, as no one can say, "Oh well, he did that for you." she did it all herself.

It was a good trip; we caught loads of fish that trip, and I had them up to over 50lb myself, with quite a few 40's. It was one of the best, if not the best winter trip – wherever we went we caught carp, it was one of those trips. The bait was working spot-on, which was a lot of it. Whereas before I might have been on the fish and just didn't get them, this time when I was on the fish, I caught them, and a lot of it was down to the bait. It was just a great, great trip, but I suppose coming home from there, the next thing was Wraysbury.

Joan with a broken leg and a personal best of 41lb 8oz!

Chapter 8
Wraysbury — Cluster's Last Stand

*"You've had Warty, so why don't you go and
fish somewhere proper, like Wraysbury?"*

It was the same old thing; I'd been fishing Colnbrook West and plodding along, trying to get Warty at 40. 'Warty the 30' didn't quite sound quite the same, but there we go. It was Simon Crow who rung me up he said, "What you doing messing about on Colnbrook West? You've caught it, blah, blah, blah... Why don't you go and have a go at somewhere proper like Wraysbury?" He said, "I've had a few goes down there and it's brilliant; you can use a boat on there, and you can fish it how you want to fish it. You can use three or four rods, get out and look for your spots, it isn't too busy on there, and it has a 50lb'er in it – Mary's in there." I thought yeah, yeah, he'd dead right; I mean, it's just a few miles down the road from where I live. But of course there was one big problem; I still had this life ban from Leisure Sports. They said it was a life ban, and they weren't joking. This was years later, and I was still banned, but by then Jack Ashford had gone, and Ian Welch had taken over. I know Joan got on with him very well, and I got on alright with him; I'd just never asked for my ticket back.

So I said to him, "How about looking at my ban? I haven't really done much wrong, so how about letting me have a ticket?" He said, "Yeah, alright, fair enough, you've been banned for about 15 years or something." It was getting on for 15 years I suppose, something like that, Christ Almighty. He said, "Yeah, it's about time you had your ticket back," so I thought, brilliant, and again I had something to channel my thoughts into – Wraysbury! I couldn't believe it – my ticket come through the letterbox, and the phone rang... Mary had died that day. I thought, how good's my luck? I wait 15 years to get a ticket, and then my ticket drops through the door on the very day that the fish I've joined for after all of that time died, which was a real shame. Mary was a fantastic fish, a lovely, lovely fish. They all go eventually, that's life, but we're all very selfish as well, and we all want to catch these fish.

But I thought to myself, well, I've got my ticket, and I still had Wraysbury in my head, so that was where I was going to fish – there were still plenty of other good fish in there. So I went down there and to be honest, I was surprised how many people were still fishing it. There were quite a few on there, considering the main fish in the lake, the famous Mary, had just died. The first day I just put my gear in the boat and I thought well, I'll just go round and round the lake, see what I can find, and just take it from there. Everyone said to me, "Look under the trees, because that's where they like to get." Well, it's 120 acres and every island is covered in trees, the whole bank is covered in trees, and I couldn't find a fish anywhere, so I set up in Dredger Bay. There are two Dredger Bay swims, and I set up in the right hand one.

Nothing happened that first night and then next day, a guy came down, one of the twins who I'd met on Fox Pool all those years earlier. I hadn't seen him for years, and I haven't seen him since, funnily enough. He just happened to turn up and he said, "Oh, hello Steve," and sat down and had a chat. Luckily, he knew a lot more about Wraysbury than I did. Well, I didn't know anything about it; I'd just gone down there, and he said, "Well, if you go out on the island and walk along, there's a spot under the trees where they do like to get at night and feed." I thought alright, so after he left I went across on the island, walked along, looked under the tree and there was one of the 40's, the Pug, sitting there under this tree with one of the stockies. I thought, Jesus, this is one of the Wraysbury 40's, and I went back and got some boilies. I thought well, I'll probably spook it, but I threw some boilies in there, and the fish went round the tree a little bit, came back, and ate them. It just went down and ate my bait – Jesus Christ, first drop of bait on the lake, and I've got a Wraysbury 40 eating my baits in front of me! The big problem obviously was that it was in the snags, which were out of bounds, so I couldn't fish for it, which is obviously why it was in there feeling safe enough to eat all my baits. But you know, it got me buzzing, there was a Wraysbury 40 eating my bait, and if it would eat my baits, obviously I had a chance of catching one.

So I went back, loaded all my gear into the boat, and moved to the left hand swim, the Little Dredger swim they call it. I thought, well, I can't get to where I saw the fish feeding, but I can get about 10-15yds away from it. There was a line of snags along this island, and you weren't allowed to fish from the start of the snags onwards, but you could fish just the side of them. So I thought, well, if they're moving up and down that bank, the best thing I can do is put a bait right in the edge by the trees. I was using four rods so I went out there and I found some lovely little clear spots, and dropped different baits, and then my fourth one, I didn't know what to do with it. It was getting a bit dark, and right in the edge, just as the bank dropped off, it was about 4-5ft deep, and there was weed on the bottom, and I just dropped it in on the weed. It was crystal clear; I could see the bait, and it just landed so that the lead went down in the weed, but the bait just rested on top. I thought that looks alright, oh sod it, that'll do, and left it at that.

I remember I was lying there, really excited because of the fish I had seen that day, and at eleven o'clock I had one bleep. I looked, and I just saw my indicator rise about half and inch, and I knew it was a take, so I literally jumped straight out behind the rod, and by the second bleep it pulled out the clip. I was so confident that I was expecting it almost. I bent into it, and this fish was obviously trying to get into the snags; it was powering away,

I moved everything over to the Little Dredger swim.

I was over the moon to see what was lying in the bottom of the net.

My Baits weren't too far from where I had seen the fish.

I scoured the lake all day long and ended up where I'd started.

and I could hear it thrash on the surface. I turned it and there was a big bay to my left, and it kited round there. I could see these big boils on the surface, and it fought hard, but I was gradually gaining line, gaining line, but as I got it near enough in front of me, it shot round left into the channel, which leads into the North Lake. I felt the line grating round all these rocks, and I knew there were some big bits of old concrete there with mussels on. I

At 44lb 7oz it was a new English best and also the biggest fish in Wraysbury 1.

didn't know what I'd hooked; I was expecting it to be one of the stockies, but it was a Wraysbury carp; you know what I mean, and I wanted one.

I held on, and it came back round. I got it into the net, and I looked in, and I thought Christ, that's one of the originals! I'll be honest; I didn't even know which one it was. I knew Mary's Mate and Mary and all that, and I'd heard of the others, but I looked at this little patch of scales, and I thought, that's got to be Cluster. I didn't know Cluster, but I thought, you're Cluster, and it was only my second night on the lake! Once again, I'd got a run early into the session, but this time I didn't lose it. I do it so many times, and for once I actually landed it, and what a fish to land! It was actually the biggest fish in Wraysbury after Mary, so it was now the biggest fish in the lake, and I'd caught it on my second night. That was very lucky obviously, even thought I'd worked for it, and I didn't just turn up, cast out and catch it. I'd found the fish, and knew what I wanted to do. but to catch it very early on is lucky in itself on a place like Wraysbury. I can understand how people feel after spending years on a lake to catch a fish, because I've done it myself. I did it on Johnsons and different lakes where I spent a lot of time, and then caught a fish, and the feeling's great. But the feeling couldn't have been any better than when I caught the fish on my second night, because I knew how good that was for me at the time. I was blown away; a Wraysbury carp was just the best it could be, and yeah, I was blown away with it – it was a mega fish.

I remember putting it on the scales, and I didn't know how big it was going to be, but it was 44lb 7oz, which was a English PB for me. I didn't know how big it was meant to be; I didn't know whether it was meant to be a mid-30, mid-40 or whatever. Other people said later that they were expecting it to be bigger, and I know it got caught twice more that year at 46lb and 48lb, so perhaps it should have been bigger, I don't know, but it didn't matter; I caught it and it was fantastic. If I never caught another English carp, to catch my PB out of any of those waters – if you catch one out of Yateley or Wraysbury, there all special aren't they? Very, very special, so that was a bit good!

Chapter 9
The Solar Years — More Mixed Bags

"Raduta, Rainbow, the St Lawrence and a new venture"

After catching Cluster out of Wraysbury, I felt like I had done my little bit of English fishing for a while. Early the next year, 2004, I went back to Raduta, and that was a good and a bad trip. We turned up to find that probably 90% the fish had died. It was just amazing how quickly Raduta came onto the scene, and how quickly it had then been wiped out. Really it was just through trying to introduce too many fish. There were loads of lovely fish in there, and it didn't need any more, but the owner had put all these fish in out of the river and they had killed everything. I was gutted, but we were there already, so there was no point in turning around and coming back home, so we carried on fishing. For the most part it was horrible; there was the smell of dead fish, and everywhere there were big mounds of earth where these fish had been buried. Thousands of them died, but there was one bit around the centre of the lake, around the hotel, where there were still a few fish being caught by the looks of it, so we moved in there for the last few days. I mean, the first week and half we'd blanked, as there was hardly anything in there to catch.

We moved in opposite the hotel and ended up catching a 56lb mirror, which was the biggest carp I'd caught out of there. The original Raduta mirrors were hard to come by; there weren't many of them in the lake, and all the years there had been all those fish in there, I'd been trying to catch one, but couldn't. Then when they were all dead, except for one left in the lake, I caught it! I mean, literally, it was the biggest fish left in the lake and it felt almost like a parting gift, because it was going to be my last trip. I knew that, but I was well pleased to catch it all the same; it was a good fish.

It was a shame, but there are always other things coming along. It was the start of Rainbow Lake 2004, which was just starting to make an impression on people. I went down there courtesy of Paul Hunt, who offered me a trip in the winter of February 2004. There was one 70lb'er in there at the time, and I thought it would be worth a go. It's amazing what's happened in the few years in between, because there are loads of big fish in there now, and they've all grown on in the last few years on the bait that's been going in. I was lucky because people are falling over themselves trying to get places on there now, and there are only so many places, but I was lucky, as I got my foot in the door early if you like before there was all this attention. So that was my first trip, in 2004. I didn't know what was going to become of Rainbow, but it was heading for great things, and more of that in a minute.

2005 was the American World Cup on the St Lawrence in the USA. I'd never fished in America before, and I hadn't fished many rivers so I was expecting probably just a great big straight river with two banks, but when

I went out there I found it's just such a lovely place, and now the St Lawrence is one of my favourite carp venues in the world. The American people really welcomed us and the fishing out there is unbelievable; you're never going to catch monsters, but you can catch millions of them and they're all wild river carp.

So we pulled a number out of the hat and looked on the map, but we didn't know what it was like or anything. We got the mouth of this bay, Whitehouse Bay and fished there. As it turned out it was the early part of June and the fish were in these bays spawning, and we just caught it right when the fish were moving in and out of the bays. We put a load of bait out, and on the third day it just all kicked off. I remember this TV crew turning up and they said, "We've interviewed everyone we can interview but we haven't seen a fish yet – we could do with a fish." So I said, "Well, most mornings we've caught one or two around this time." I saw my rod tip go, and I said, "Get the camera, my rod tips going; we've got one," and then it roared off. Well it was the start of this shoal of fish moving in, and for the next seven hours, we just never stopped catching carp. In that time we caught 800lb of fish or something; it was a joke! The people who were weighing the fish just stayed behind us, and we just kept passing them, and they were putting them back. We built up a lead that was never going to get caught basically, so we won. We doubled the weight of the team in second place, which was alright! We were the first people to win a world championship twice, and won't go too much further into that other than to say it was just a really good time.

I got voted International Carp Angler of the Year two years running in 2004 and 2005, so that was a result, and I got a grand out of the old magazines for that, which always helps. It's an honour to get voted I suppose, but there are plenty of other people out there catching as many as me who just doesn't get mentioned in the mags as much.

As for the English fishing, I didn't do too much that year. I did a bit on Mayfields Lake, which was probably the closest I've ever fished to home. I know when that first got stocked you came down and did a little feature on it and there were loads in there. They were nice fish, weren't they? They were stocked out of Stockley Park; they started to grow on, and there were a few originals in there. To be honest, I could do an underarm chuck from my front door into the lake; it was about 50m from my front door, so I should have done more on there. I've done the odd little bit on there, and did a bit of film with Rob Hughes, who has got his own TV programme with Sky, and I had a few little sessions over there. That's what we've used Mayfields for, although to be fair, it's a better lake than that. It's a nice little lake in its own right, but it's an ideal little venue for doing features on because you can go down and catch a few fish.

I've caught a few up to around 30lb out of there, some good looking fish, and what I do like about Mayfields is the floater fishing. I haven't done much floater fishing in the last few years, but when it's nice, they do have it on Mayfields. When the World Cup was on, I was going to come back and watch the England game, but I thought I'd nip over there and do an hour's fishing. It was just one of those days when they were having it – I missed

Any moment now! Ready for action in swim 18 at Rainbow.

Almost certainly the biggest fish in the lake at 56lb.

Another day session down at Cassien, and I'm in to a good fish just after moving swims.

One of Cassien's jewels, the fish known as 'Fleur' at 51lb 12oz.

A big summer common from the north arm.

In 2004 I went to Rainbow Lake for the first time. It was soon to become the world's best big fish water.

In April 2005 I caught this previously unknown monster of 68lb 4oz! It is now the biggest fish in the lake.

Another of the big Rainbow mirrors seen here at 57lb.

Closer to home (about 50 metres away in fact) and a Mayfield mirror of 29lb 13oz.

the England game, and in one afternoon I hooked 20. I landed 16 and lost four up to good 20's, but it was a proper good afternoon's floater fishing. I don't think I've ever had that many in one day, probably not in a season half the time, and there were some nice pretty fish amongst the old Mayfield fish. So yeah, I enjoyed that, and all on little chopped down pop-ups. What I noticed with the Mayfield fish was that I tried using artificial baits and they wouldn't even look at them – the artificial bread and all that. I thought I'd put a bit of that on the hook and fool them, but they wouldn't look at it; they just swam straight underneath it and didn't take a blind bit of notice, but as soon as you put a bit of pop-up on or something, they'd have it.

I suppose after that came a bit of business really. I'd always got on well with Rob Hughes, and I had enjoyed doing a bit of filming with Simon Crow for Sky TV. Something always seemed to happen when we were filming together; we'd catch fish, but we just seemed to get on alright, and I fished with Simon a fair old bit. They mentioned to me that they were thinking about starting up a tackle company, and would I be interested in going in with them. I thought, yeah, as I was looking to move on a bit myself. I'd worked for six or eight years, or probably a bit more than that, for other companies, with Hutchinson and bits and pieces here and there, and I felt it was time to move on and be in control of my own destiny a bit more. So we all got together and started up Venture Tackle, and we had a good idea what we wanted to do. We wanted to bring out a range of tackle that was more top end, as there was a lot of tat around on the market, and we all knew ourselves what we wanted to use.

We all felt that there were only a few bits out there that really suited what we wanted to use ourselves. There was loads of stuff out there that wasn't quite right, and we thought to ourselves if we do our own company, we'll make the stuff exactly right for how we want to use it, and hopefully that would be what everyone else wants to use as well, and so far, it's proved to be right. We've done so much fishing over the years, and when you use things you think, well, it's great but if only it had this little thing a bit different, or it was a bit bigger here, or a bit different there, it would be spot on – well that's what we set out to do.

So we haven't got a big range of gear, as the idea was to make good quality, very usable gear; gear that we would want to use ourselves, and see where we go. So far the response has been really good and it's quite exciting to actually move into that area instead of working for someone else. It's a big thing to take on, and anyone who's in the business reading this will know what I mean. You think it's going to be a lot easier than it is; it's actually very hard, and there's a lot of competition out there, but at the same it's great to see ideas come from bits of paper and drawings and diagrams into samples, and then into finished products and into shops, and then see people buying those products and saying how good they are. It gives you a real buzz to think you've done something good, and hopefully we'll make loads of money out of it, but that certainly isn't the case at the moment. It's a tough business, and you've got to work really hard at it and be on the ball all the time to get anywhere, but at the same time, it's very enjoyable, so we're a good little team. We knew each other before, and they say don't mix business and friends, but we've done that and it works alright, so let's hope it continues. If it goes the same way as it's going at the moment, we'll all carry on and be happy at the end of the day. It's nice to be involved in the fishing business and be involved with friends. To me, it's the perfect scenario, so we're all happy with it, and let's keep it going.

The other thing is, we moved on from Rod Hutchinson, and joined Solar Products. Martin Locke had been a friend for years; he'd always been around, so we all joined forces with him at the same time. Rod Hutchinson had been great, very easy going, and great to work with, and his baits were brilliant, and still are, but it was just time to move on. Martin's got a very inventive mind, and we all know how good his gear is, so we were all happy to move in and start promoting and using his gear because it's great. I think our companies work very well hand-in-hand because Martin's very innovative, and when you look at his stainless gear and indicators and all that, everyone agrees they're the best out there. Venture are also coming up with great ideas like the Razor Back Bivvy, which everyone's copying now, which is a bit frustrating, but it's also a compliment to the ideas that we've come up with. So I think Venture and Solar products work well together, but they don't conflict with each other. We've both got our individual ranges, but it's nice to have that association, so it's very exciting businesswise. So that's the most exciting thing that's happened to me for... probably forever... we're all as mad keen now as we were, and yeah it's great stuff.

Fishing-wise, blimey, I'm still going everywhere. As time's gone on I've just gone more and more to fishing abroad. I've always wanted to fish in England more than I have done, but at the same time, I love fishing abroad. Every trip abroad is an experience of its own, and you could write a book on a two-week session, whereas a year's fishing on an English water can go by, and you've had two fish, and there's not much to write about. Most people just expect me to write about foreign fishing and I've come to rely on the money that I get from writing about foreign fishing, so it's almost come to be a job. I've got to go away to keep writing the articles to keep

A good day's floater fishing on Mayfield – just one of 16 carp that afternoon!

A quick couple of nights on Colnbrook West and an English PB common of 35lb 10oz.

Our good friend Gary Hillson cooking up a winter meal on the banks of Cassien.

What could be better on Christmas Day? A 45lb mirror.

I hadn't fished many commercial lakes but this 56lb mirror from Lac Serreire made the effort worthwhile.

Our swim for the 2005 World Carp Cup on the St. Lawrence River in the USA

the money coming in, and I'd need two lifetimes to do it all, so something has to give, and it's the English fishing that's given a bit.

I went to Austria with Joan and Crowie, and what a trip that was. We went to Kurt Grabmayer's lake, and we all caught 50lb'ers. Joan got in first again with a 51lb common; I was out in the boat this time, and heard a few bleeps. I thought, what's going on, and saw Joan with a rod in her hand, and I thought I'd better get back to the bank. As I was going towards Joan, I went past this big common going along on the surface, heading towards Joan, and I thought, that's big as well. I got the bank, netted it, and it was 51½lb, so she'd done it again. Later in the week I had a 55lb 10oz common, which is still my personal best, and Crowie had a 50lb 10oz mirror, so it was an amazing week's fishing really. That was my fourth country that I'd caught a 50 from, which no one had done at the time. Alijn Danau's done it since, but he's the only other one we know of, so it's a bit of a race to be the first one with five countries. I'm still trying to get an English one at the moment, or a Belgian one, or anywhere really... Spanish – that'll do.

I had a few more Cassien trips, which were again very good, but as for English fishing, I started fishing Stockley Lake with Rob Hughes, which is another local Boyer Leisure water. I did a bit of fishing here and there on a very exclusive Colne Valley water, which I don't really want to say too much about while I'm still trying to catch from there. The main fish I was after got caught, and I saw it on the bank, and oh, what a fish; it's lovely. I want to catch that, but then I was left in limbo, and wondered what to do. All of a sudden Stockley had a 40lb'er in there, and not only that, it was six weeks into the season and this 40lb'er had been caught five times, so I rang Rob up. He was living in Uxbridge; he's just about to move again, but he was living in Uxbridge at the time, and I said, "Rob, this little lake down the road, Stockley, it's only round the corner, and there's a 40 in there, which has been caught five times in six weeks. How do you fancy going down there for a couple of nights? We'll whack it out." He said, "Yeah, sounds alright to me."

The second night I was on there, I didn't take my scales with me, but I had this fully scaled mirror of about 26-27lb, a lovely looking fish. Rob came down a couple of nights later, and had a common of 33lb and another one of 27lb. We didn't know about all these fish, and there were obviously more really good-looking fish in there than we thought, so we started fishing it. Rob, to be fair, was catching more than me; he really got it off to a fine art, and he was getting a fish every single night, whereas I was only getting one every two or three nights. It was the same old story; they'd tell us that it had been caught just before we arrived, or just after we left. Actually I'm talking about Gertie here –Gertie the Forty. It used to be Gertie the Thirty, but all of a sudden Gertie was a 40, whereas the other one, Warty the Forty, I caught at 30...

It was just one of those things, but, what we did find out later was that the fully scaled I caught was the biggest fully scaled in the lake, and the common Rob caught the first night he was on there was the biggest common in the lake. So you know, there were a lot more smaller fish in there than we first thought, but they were lovely fish, and we still hadn't caught Gertie. I did the start of the season on there, and I thought, right, it's the start of season, and like Warty previously, there was a good chance of catching it. We went down there, and there were eleven fish caught; I caught nine of them, and the other two were only like 9lb or 10lb, little ones, but the biggest one I caught was 23lb. I went home and a guy moved into my swim and that night he had the big'un at 41lb, and a big 30 to go with it. If you're not meant to catch them, you won't, but I could go back tonight and whack it out; it's one of those fish. I'll keep trying anyway.

Also I had a session on Acton Burnell in September. I'd met Rob Hales down on Rainbow, and it wasn't a water I'd ever really intended fishing, or wanted to fish or anything, but he said, "Come up for a guest session for a few nights here and there if you want." Normally you're only allowed to do two nights on there, but he said come up for four or five nights if I wanted. I liked him; he seemed a nice bloke, so I went up there. There was one other guy on there, who packed up as we arrived, so we had the lake to ourselves, and fish were jumping out in front of us. To cut a long story short, on the third night I had a bite and got a 40lb 10oz common, which is the biggest common I've caught in England. It was great; I was pleased to catch it, and it's a lovely lake.

So that was my bit of fishing for that year, which really brings us more or less up to the present day. I've had some fantastic fishing; I had a trip to Canada just a few months ago, at the end of last year, on the St Lawrence, and that was just mental. I caught 117 carp in five days, and loads of 30's – nothing big, but it was very good fishing. Morocco came on the scene, and that was the new big fish water, so I had a trip out there with Crowie, and we were the first English people to set foot on there and fish it. I caught one, so I was the first English bloke to catch a fish out of the lake, which doesn't mean a lot, but it was quite pleasing all the same.

I suppose Rainbow is the water I got involved with because big fish were starting to come out of there, and it quickly became the best big fish water in the world. It will never be what Cassien is; Cassien will always be my favourite water abroad, but when there are all those big fish in there, and

First decent fish of the competition, a 31½ lb common.

The action just got better and better throughout the five days.

That winning moment – "You have the glasses, chaps – I'll just keep the bottle!"

It was just a fantastic moment and one that will stay with me forever.

once you see a few of them on the bank, it gets you going back for more. In 2005 I caught a 68lb'er, which actually beat my long-standing personal best that I'd had from Cassien all those years before. It took me 18 years to beat my Cassien fish, and then I caught this 68lb'er from Rainbow, which amazingly was unknown before that capture. You know, I wondered how big it had been before, and so I showed everyone, including Pascal the owner, but none of them had seen it before. Obviously it must have been caught before at some stage, but no one has ever produced a picture of it before. That's now gone on to be the biggest fish in the lake; a year later it was 82lb, and that's the sort of thing that happens at Rainbow – it's an incredible water, and it does keep me going back; I still have two or three trips there every year.

This year I went back in June; it went off the second day, and I hooked into what was definitely a great big fish. It rolled twice at the net, and I thought it was at least 50, probably quite a bit bigger, and the hook popped out. I sat there for two hours, and I couldn't speak; it was a big fish definitely, and it would have been the biggest fish of the year for me up to that point. I put the rod back out and the same one went off again. I thought I'd better go out in the boat to make sure with this one, and I didn't think it was that big, but I got it up and thought Christ, that is big. That one was 68lb 8oz, a PB by 4oz, so I was well pleased with that. A few days later, the same rod went off again with a 70lb 8oz on the end, so you know… It's the best big fish water in the world, and they do get caught, but you still get the view that it's easier than it actually is. When you're actually there fishing, it doesn't matter which water those big fish in; you've still got to work hard for them, and you know, I have worked hard. I've had quite a few trips there now for those fish, and I've always wanted a 70lb'er. I always wanted it to come from Cassien, but you know, I'll have one from wherever it wants to come from really, and when I saw that needle go past 70lb – yes, I'd done it at last! All these years – 30-odd years of carp fishing, and I'd caught a 70lb'er at last. I mean to put it in perspective, in 33 years of carp fishing I'd caught one fish over 30kg, and I caught two that week alone, so you know, that's how good that week was, and there was another big fish that fell off as well. It was great, but having achieved what I wanted to do there, I'll still go back. But I'd achieved what I wanted to do at Rainbow, and the good old Club Mix boilies did it for me there. Before it was the old MC Addicted that did it, and now it's the old Club Mix – I've caught a lot of big fish now on the Club Mix.

Chapter 10
The Mere — The Last Capture of the Black Mirror

"You always have to fish under cover with a minimum of gear. Bivvies are out of the question"

The first time I saw any fish there as such was 2006. I'd never seen The Black Mirror; I'd seen a couple of commons in the past, and actually one of the first fish I saw was this massive common. It was around June time, and I walked all round the lake a couple of times. I'd just got to this little corner at the top end, and you know sometimes when you just look at somewhere, and you think, well, if there's going to be a fish, there's gonna be one here. I saw nothing for a couple of minutes, and then this fish moved across. I got up a tree in the corner and this common was just sitting there. I remember looking at it for about four or five minutes before it dawned on me just how big it was, and I thought, Christ, that's a big common. It was there for a while, then another fish started to come and go, and then The Black Mirror actually came in next to it. Knowing how big The Black Mirror was, that it was over 50lb; this common was the same sort of size. I presume this was the common that other people have seen, but it was a very light fish, not a dark one. People have always talked about a big, dark common, but I never saw a big, dark common in there.

I saw this light one probably half a dozen times, always in the same area. It was big, but as far as I know it's never been caught or even been hooked. It was one of the mysteries of The Mere really, I suppose, and one of the things that just makes you want to fish it. No one else seemed to be fishing that area of the lake, and I thought well, The Black Mirror's here, and the big common's here. So what I did was bait up all the areas in the margin up that end of the lake – there was about seven areas that looked good. There was a lot of weed about, and I just baited up these areas and came back the next day or a couple of days later just to see what had happened. Well six of the areas were untouched, and they looked perfect areas – little gravel spots under bushes 5ft or 6ft from where I was seeing the fish. I expected them to go, but the only spot that actually got touched was the one furthest away from where I'd seen the fish, and that had got cleared. I didn't expect it to happen like that; I'd only been there seven or eight nights by then, and I kept looking at it thinking it is gone isn't it? I was trying to convince myself, but in the end I thought, no, the bait has gone; it's not there.

So that night I put a rod in there, laid under the brambles on the floor like you do, and at midnight, it hammered off. I lost the fish, and I only had it on for a few seconds, but it frightened the life out of me really. At the time I wasn't that disappointed, I think because I'd expected to wait longer for a bite and I'd got one quite quickly. It was my ninth or tenth night, and although I'd lost it I thought, well, I know what I'm doing now – this isn't going to be that hard after all. That was probably my first lesson, because I came back the following week, the water had turned green, and I couldn't see any of the spots any more, but you know; that was The Mere. Every time you think you've found a clue it would put a brick wall in front of you, something would change, and the opportunities were very, very few and far between. They changed very quickly as well – just when you thought you'd got something going, it would change. That was my one chance for a long, long time that was.

So yeah, that would have been 2006. Probably the other thing that held me back with it so long is that when it got caught, I stopped fishing there for a while. That was a big mistake looking back, because I was never there just for The Black Mirror. I mean there are people who are there that only want to catch that fish and none of the others, whereas I always said to myself that I'd have any of them. A Mere carp is a Mere carp, and The Black Mirror is definitely top of the tree; it's the ultimate fish, but they're all special, and I'd have any of them – 10lb'ers, 50lb'ers, whatever... So, I'd generally pull off the lake for a while, and that was a mistake. There are normally one or two chances of that fish in a year, and if it got caught, quite often it would be one of the first fish caught. There might only be six fish caught in a year, which was often the case, and if The Black Mirror was the first or second one out and I pulled off, I was missing out on the chance of catching one of the others and just learning about the place.

So you know, I sort of held myself back there a bit, and generally I used to go off and fish some of the other waters if The Black Mirror had been out. I used to go up to Stockley, which was a nice little lake. It's got some nice old fish in it still, some of the old originals, and I've had some good times on there. I'm not going go into all the fishing I did over the last couple of years, but I did concentrate on The Mere, and then fitted everything else in around it. It gradually became more and more important, and I probably wasn't putting in enough time there. Looking back, after fishing The Mere for the time I did, what's obvious is that you've got to give it everything; it's no good going in half-heartedly. The first two or three years I was probably doing 20 nights a year, and it wasn't enough, as the chances are so few and far between. Most days you'd see a fish show or something, but generally nothing would happen, and you'd feel like you were just going through the motions, but without doing that, you wouldn't be there at the time when those little windows of opportunity open up. That's what they were – windows of opportunity in amongst lots of nothingness...

So I'd be doing lots of time, and every now and then a little window would open up. It was one thing recognising when that little window of opportunity opened up, but another thing taking advantage of it. As time went on, I was able to do that more and more, and it was from just putting

Set up for a few days on Chad Lakes' Home Pool.

I had a few nights spare for Stockley and found the carp in a friendly mood.

Cottington Lakes were a pleasant surprise, and I came away with a new surface PB of 33lb 8oz.

in more time and just knowing the lake better, I suppose. It was without a doubt the hardest fishing I've ever done in my life; it's the hardest thing I've ever done in my life, full stop. I've never worked so hard for fishing or anything; it's incredibly hard, and I never really found a way of fishing there that I was comfortable with, because you're not meant to be there. You always had to fish undercover with the minimum of gear – bivvies and things like that are out of the question, so there were no comforts, and just getting in and out of there with your gear was hard. There were times when you could come and go, like early morning and late at night when you were obviously safe, but you always felt a bit strange. I always felt a bit on edge coming and going there, and I tried different things. I tried stashing gear down there, but that either got eaten by the mice, or waterlogged and damp, or just got nicked. I had loads of gear nicked and tampered with, but I didn't want to be walking in and out of there with too much gear. It was difficult to find a comfortable way of fishing it, and I never did really; it was just hard work. Just getting round the place is hard, as it's so overgrown, and if you saw a fish jump at the other end, you'd end up ripped to pieces carrying all your gear through the brambles, but you know, it's what you had to do, or otherwise why be there? Yeah, very, very tough fishing, but fantastic – the most enjoyable fishing I've ever done in my life, I should think.

I was still travelling abroad a lot, and still doing my bits and pieces and trying to fit The Mere in between all that. Of course what would happen was that I'd go away, come back, and The Black Mirror had been caught; it always seemed to happen like that. So the only way I was going to do it was to just dedicate more time to it, and last year, after that last interview we did, I thought right, now I'm going to concentrate; the Mere's going to be the main place I'm going to fish. I cancelled several trips abroad at the times when I thought it was going to be due out, and just decided to give it my best shot.

I think in the spring of last year I had one week away and it got caught while I was away, so it was Sod's Law that it happened again. I got back on the Monday, and there was no one there. It was quite often that I was the only one on the place, but I bumped into one guy and he said, "Oh you know it came out Saturday," and my heart sank. I thought well, this time I'm not pulling off; I'm just going to carry on. I know there's always a chance of catching it again; it has been caught once soon after being caught before, but generally it's not going to happen. I still hadn't caught a carp out of there, and I still needed to catch a Mere carp, so I just kept going and going. I baited up all these different little spots, and I was just pulling off one day. I'd stashed my gear because there were a couple of people around who I didn't like the look of. I didn't know who they were, and it was time to make myself scarce if you know what I mean. I was just walking off and I thought, right, I'll check one of my baited spots on the way out. I got up the tree, looked down, and all the bait was gone, and just as I was watching a mid-30 common come through and my legs went to jelly. Even after all these years of catching fish and all that, my legs went to jelly, and I just knew that was my chance. I was filled with excitement, but I couldn't fish there and then. I wanted to get my rod, but it was a bit dodgy, so I thought, I'm coming back tonight. I literally sat at home drinking tea and my hands were shaking. I kept looking at my watch and it was a minute after the last time I'd looked, but I just knew that was going to be it.

So I got back there about 10pm and put a bait on the spot. It was literally just under the rod tip, and I remember sitting bolt upright at 4am looking at my watch thinking, oh no, it hasn't happened. I lay back on my bedchair, shut my eyes, and it absolutely hammered off. I tell you how confident I was; I'd actually slept in my chest waders that night. I'd waded out and dropped this bait, and just got in the sleeping bag with my chest waders on because I knew I was going to be getting a bite. This was my 63rd night on

I caught a few carp at Cottington including this mid-20.

I didn't think I'd ever fish Redmire but I'm so pleased I went there – it was the water I'd dreamed of fishing in the 1970's.

It doesn't hold the monsters it once did but every Redmire carp is special.

the lake; there were loads of nights where you just knew you weren't going to catch, and the odd nights where I felt confident, but it still never happened. But that night it was going to happen, and it did happen. You don't know how you're going feel until you actually catch one; you play it through your mind so many times catching that fish, jumping up and down and swinging round trees, but when I got it in the net it was just a relief. I didn't jump up and down; it was like, oh thank God. I should have caught one earlier – that's probably the feeling I had – it was overdue, but I'd caught one, I'd caught a Mere carp. It was 20lb 8oz, and the best fish by a long way that I caught that year. I thought whatever happens at least I've caught one out of this lake after all that time – it justified it a bit.

As always, the first one is generally the most difficult one, and it just gave me that confidence, I went from someone hoping to catch a Mere carp to someone who had caught a Mere carp. It's a difficult lake to catch them from, but they're still carp, and I could catch them, so it was a bit of a milestone.

As before, a week later the water went green, and I couldn't see the spot any more. I was just thankful that I'd made the most of that opportunity because I could have gone home earlier, or not looked at that spot, and might have missed it all. The bait might still have been there, or I might not have seen the fish. Those little things make such a difference on there – just seeing those opportunities. But I'd caught one anyway, and as the summer went on, the fish moved out of the edge. There are little periods on there where you can catch the fish in the edge, but they're so brief, and all of a sudden they're gone again. Then you entered periods where you just don't see anything for weeks, and you think, well I know they're out there, but where are they? So you start fishing open water spots, as you think if you're not seeing them in the edge they've got to be out there somewhere.

That's basically what I started doing, and I did really struggle to get any action in the open water. It was so difficult to actually find areas where I felt like it was the spot; you know, when you cast out and it goes down donk – that never happened. There were so many spots where it goes down in the weed and you think, no, that's not the spot – there was loads of that. There was one spot I found where it went down deeper than the rest, so it wasn't ideal, but because it was deeper it was a bit clearer. I just kept putting bait on that spot because it was one of the few clear spots I could find out there. I just kept baiting it and baiting it every time I was there, and gradually, over time, even though I never saw a fish show, the spot seemed to become smoother and harder. I thought it had to be fish clearing the bait; it's the only thing that would make it smoother and harder.

Eventually when it came to September time, I had two bites in a week off that spot. I had a 29lb 12oz common, and a week later I had a 38lb 4oz common, and they were both on hinged stiff rigs. I said earlier I couldn't get on with the chod rig, which is ideal in theory for fishing down there with conditions they way they are. Most of the guys were on it, but it just didn't work for me. I kept plugging away with the hinged stiff rig, because it had always worked for me on other waters, and eventually that was what I had those two fish on; little pop-ups out on that clear, smooth spot.

Looking through the history of The Black Mirror, people think of the fishing down there as mainly margin stuff, fishing on the clear spots, or at least that's what a lot of people tend to talk about. The big'un itself though, has been caught more from open water than anywhere else, so it tends to drag you into that type of fishing, I know Steve Pagulatos caught it years ago in the edge under the rod tip, and there are probably a few other captures that I don't know the full story of, but in general, most captures were from fishing out in open water. For that reason, I always thought that was the way to catch it, and there were also certain swims on there that it comes out of more than any others. So probably most of the fishing I did was in the open water, but those two commons in that week were the only two bites I ever had fishing that way. It's swings and roundabouts I suppose, and fishing to your strengths, to what you know, is so important when you're fishing in those sorts of waters for those sorts of fish. It's no good trying to follow the crowd; I mean you know as well as anyone else that when you're fishing for those fish you've got to go in with a rig and a bait that you're perfectly confident in and stick with it. If you do change, change for your own reasons, not because you've seen someone else fishing a different way and think, oh, maybe that's the way.

You've got to be so clear in your mind about what you're doing because it's just such difficult fishing. Rigs and bait do come into it, but it's all about your own mindset – the confidence and willpower and the strength of character of the people fishing for these fish. That's why certain people like Tel, Jim Shelley, Nigel Sharp and Darrell Peck are very successful at fishing for these big fish; they've got that tunnel vision and a mindset and strength of character to go after them. There are a lot of them around now, and they're all very strong willed people, and you need to be like that – that's what that fishing demands of you.

So that was the end of last year, 2009. I had also lost another fish, so I'd had four bites that year, and landed three fish, which for The Mere is a proper result. If you catch one or two fish, you've done well, so three was great, and at last I felt like I knew what I was doing. When it came to this year, 2010, I knew what I was looking for, and I knew that when the opportunities arose I was going to be there and ready for them. The other thing that changed this year was that after catching the fish, I felt so much more confident in my own ability. The first couple of years on there, there were people who I was sure were going to catch The Black Mirror, and I wasn't one of them, if you know what I mean. I was hoping to get a fish or two, but when I think back to the first year, Si Baker was on there (I hope he doesn't mind me mentioning his name), and when I watched him fishing and talked to him, to my mind he was the one who was going to catch it. He was so confident in his own ability and he was so on the ball. I remember him saying to me one time, "It's imminent; it's going to be out," and I thought, blimey is it? Well, the next week he'd caught it, and I thought bloody hell.

But in 2010, all of a sudden I felt in my own mind that I was in pole position to catch it, and if anyone was going to catch it, it was going to be me. I was putting in more time than probably anyone else. If it was being seen, I was seeing it, and I was getting myself into positions where it was. I mean any one of those anglers could have caught it, but I felt like I was the most likely, which give me so much confidence.

I think there had been one fish out early on, but it was a very slow start to the year. The 2009/10 winter was dreadful; it just dragged on and on, and I started down there in March. I always used to do a few nights in March anyway, because there was never anyone there in March, but there were always things happening. I'd either get liners or I'd see fish showing, and it was just lovely to be down there on my own when other people weren't there. I just felt like it gave me an edge to be on there before everyone else. Nothing ever happened in March; I never caught one in March, but I still saw them this year – I just never got a bite.

I've got a bit carried away with myself here; I'm almost up to the spring of 2010 and there are a few bits I've missed out. There's some fishing I did last year, and a few of the places I've been to that I wanted to talk about. I've got so involved, but The Mere always does that to me; I love the place so much that once I start talking about it, I can't stop. But there are a few things and a few fish I would just like to mention, so I'll step back a little bit.

For a start, I fished Redmire Pool for the first time last year. I was only up there for three nights, but for me it was such an important event in my life. The reason being that when I started carp fishing in the 1970's, Redmire was the place, and you know I'd grown up reading about it in Angling Times and the fishing papers of those days. It was all about Jack Hilton – my time was a bit after Dick Walker, but Jack Hilton was the man in those days, and Redmire Pool was the place in those days. I never had a chance of fishing it, but I'd always dreamed I would. As years went by, of course the chance came up that people could fish it, but then I thought to myself, well, those big fish aren't there any more, and the place isn't going to be what it was in those days. I didn't want to spoil the illusion of Redmire, the illusion that I had in my head of the place in those early years. I didn't want to go there and look at the place and think, oh, is this it? So for one reason or another, I never went to fish there.

Then a chance came up. Tim Paisley was up there; he had the lake for two weeks, and he phoned me up and said, "I'm up here, you can come up for a few nights if you want." I thought about it and I thought, yeah, I should go up there and fish it just to see this place that was such a big part of my life in the early years of my carp fishing. I decided to do a couple of nights, and why not, as I might have regretted it if I hadn't gone. I've got to say that when I actually did go there, it blew me away. It had quite an impact on me because I think it has actually changed so little over the years. Just walking on there, especially walking on the dam wall, you know it looked virtually the same because you see so many pictures of the dam wall from years ago going back to the Walker years, and before then even. You walk along that dam wall and you can picture all those people – Jack Hilton, Dick Walker and Fred J Taylor, and it was lovely to go and relive all that history. I mean the fishing there isn't about big fish now; if you catch a 30 there, you've really caught a big'un. It's more about stepping back in time and reliving a bit of that history, and fishing swims that my heroes from 35 years ago fished. In that way it was lovely to go up there, and I did catch a couple of carp. Of course once you're there, the next important step is actually catching a Redmire carp. I caught a mirror and a common, not big, just doubles. I caught a lovely little scaly mirror on the first night. Yeah, it's hard to explain to some people I suppose, but to me it was a special moment, because it was like I'd caught one from the water that meant so much to me in the past, so it was lovely, and I really, really enjoyed my few days on Redmire.

There's one place I fished last year that I'd never heard of before – Cottington Lakes, down near Dover somewhere. I'd never heard of the place, and it only came about because we were doing a day in the shop with Venture. Dave, who had organised this, was very good at finding a local lake in the area, and he said, "We'll do the day in the shop, and I've found this lake down the road, Cottington Lakes, and we can do the night there and the next day." So, we spent a night there, and I didn't really enjoy it too much. Nothing happened until 2am when one went off, and I caught this 25lb fully scaled mirror, which was a stunner. I thought that's a right result, catching a fish like that, and a couple of the blokes came over and said, "Oh yeah, they all look like that in here; there are loads of scaly fish." I thought, Jesus Christ, and they said, "There are quite a few 30's as well," and I thought blimey, that's alright then. It opened up my eyes, and I wondered how I'd never heard of it before.

Anyway, it got quite warm, I was fishing by this weedbed, and I'm a bit like you; I love the floater fishing. I probably don't do it as much as I should do, but I thought I'd fire some mixers out to see what happened by this weed bed. It all looked quite dead actually, but literally as soon as these mixers went out, about half a dozen mouths came up. I didn't even know they were there until they just appeared, and they obviously liked the mixers. So obviously I set my rod up straight away, and although it looked easy, it's never as easy as you think it's going to be, is it? You put the bait out there; they're always taking them about a foot away, and you think the hookbait's next, but then they come up a foot to the other side and start taking them. But eventually I hooked into this fish, and it was a good old battle. I've never caught that many big fish off the top, and it was a surface caught PB for me at 33lb 8oz, a lovely linear, another stunning fish – brilliant. I've actually seen a picture of that fish in Carp-Talk this year at over 40lb. We were only there for the day, so I packed up and went home in the afternoon, but I caught another two or three fish before I went – a mid-20 and a high double, again lovely, scaly fish. I've not been back there since, but I tell you what, if you love scaly carp like the Horseshoe fish, then Cottington Lakes is well worth a go. I will go back there one day because it was a fantastic place, and just totally under the radar.

Well, all I've talked about is the English fishing so far, but there was still a Cassien winter trip. I hadn't been to Cassien for the last couple of winters; I was ill one year, and then Joan was ill the following year, so we never made it to Cassien for our regular winter trip that we had done for years. So last winter, December 2009, we got back there for a couple of weeks. We drove from Belgium, as I'd just done a show there for the release of my book so I literally had to drive from there all the way down to Cassien, but it was lovely to be back there. I absolutely love Cassien and the winter trips because normally I wouldn't be doing too much over in England in December, so it's the perfect time to have a trip down there, and I ended up catching four fish. The first three fish were all 40's up to 47lb, which was nice anyway, and then I was woken up on Christmas morning by a screaming run from a 26lb common. It's what Cassien's all about – fantastic – so I

My old mate Crowy with Black Eye at somewhere around mid-50's.

In difficult conditions I caught a Home Pool carp of 28lb 4oz.

The fish picked up the bait right beside that tuft of grass.

Back at Cassien for December 09 and it was as good as ever. This was one of three 40's in just over a week.

Enjoying the December sunshine with friends at Cassien.

Christmas morning, and what could be better that having a carp to photograph?

Sometimes I had the luxury of a bedchair if I could keep out of the way.

really, really enjoyed that.

And getting onto this year, one little place that's been in the news a lot in the last few years is Chad Lakes' Home Pool, which was somewhere I hadn't fished before. I didn't think I'd ever get to fish it really, as it wasn't high on my list of places to go, but my good mate Simon Crow had two weeks booked on there. He was after Black Eye, and he knew from the year before that it had been caught two or three times during that week, so he booked them with the aim of catching it in the time he was there. Well, he turned up and he caught it within the first six hours of being there, which surprised him and most other people. It's been put on the bank a few times in the past, but it's a proper English one, a big mid-50, but it hasn't been so easy this year. Simon just happened to be in the right place at the right time; the fish were feeding, clouding up, and he dropped a bait in there. Probably half a dozen fish could have picked up the bait but he got the right one. He got Black Eye, but of course that left him with the best part of two weeks, having already caught his target fish, so he made me the offer that if I wanted to have a few days up there with the permission of the owner, Dave Ayres, I could have a couple of days on there.

It was something I wasn't going to turn down, because it's an English 50, and I wanted to catch an English 50. It wasn't the one I most wanted to catch, obviously, but I wasn't going to shake it off at the net if I hooked it because it's a lovely fish, a proper pedigree fish. When it's on the munch it comes out a bit, which sort of detracts from the capture in some people's eyes, but like I said, I wasn't going to shake it off if I had a chance. So I shot up there for three nights, and literally within five minutes of walking round there I'd found Black Eye. Home Pool is probably only an acre and half, and it's a lovely place, a lovely little pool, and I enjoyed fishing it. You can't miss Black Eye; it was sitting in this weedbed, probably sulking after it had been caught. After he caught the fish, Crowy said that's where it went. I fished it for three nights, and you'd wake up in the morning and see its back in the weedbed, and go to bed at night and it would still be there. So you know, I didn't really feel like I had any chance of catching it, but I had a bait as near as I could get to it anyway.

It's just a nice style of fishing up there; it's all very intimate, close range stuff. Conditions weren't really right when I went there; it had turned a little bit chilly. We were seeing the fish; they aren't hard to see, but Crowy said to me, "Just find where they're clouding up and put a bit of bait in there with your hookbait." Well, I was finding fish, but they weren't clouding up and feeding, so it was a little bit tricky. On the final day, I did find one little spot right in the edge by this little tuft of grass up towards the house. I looked down there and there was a koi of about mid-20's probably and a mirror about the same size clouding up in the edge. I waited until they just moved out a little bit, dropped a bait in there, and expected to get a bite in about half an hour. I sneaked back and had a little look and they were still there clouding up, but it didn't go off. In the end it was actually the next morning at about 3.15 that one hammered off.

It's funny with that type of fishing sometimes, you see fish clouding up, you drop a bait right in there and literally the bait's in front of their noses and you think it's got to go off quickly, but it doesn't; it's about twelve hours later you get a bite, but that's just the way it happens. Sometimes you can be too impatient; you can try for an hour and think they're not going to have it, the fish move off and you take that rod away. Well leave it there, as sometimes they come back and have it, which was what happened. It was a 28lb mirror in the end, not Black Eye, but I was pleased to get one out of there. When people talk about Chad Lakes' Home Pool you think oh, that's quite easy that place, fish get caught from there all the time. But he keeps a catch report book there so all the catches are in there. Basically the lake's split into two halves; there's a larger end and a narrower end, split by two islands. It was April and there had been 13 fish caught during the year up until that point. So there hadn't been loads of fish getting caught at all, and 12 of those 13 had been caught from the wider end. The guy who had booked the lake with Crowy was still there fishing, so obviously he had the wider end, which was fair enough. I had the narrow end, and it wasn't until I looked through the book that I realised there's only been one fish caught from that end of the lake all year. So even though I was seeing the fish there, it wasn't easy, but I'd got one, so I was well happy with that. It was only the second one from up that end, so it turned out to be a better capture than it seemed really, and I was happy enough with it. It's always nice when you go to a lake to actually catch a fish, and then go away saying you've had one. Black Eye was still in his weedbed when I left, and by the sound of it he stayed there for a few more weeks. He's a great old fish, and it was nice to see him anyway.

But that sort of brings us up to speed a bit on where I'd left off with The Mere, because that was late April. As soon as you go anywhere even for a couple of days, you're just terrified that the phone will ring or a text message is going to come through saying, "It's been out while you've been away." But there were no text messages or anything, and the weather was just starting to warm up. It was that period where the long winter was finally over, the sunshine was coming through and the water was starting to warm up. The Mere is quite a deep water; it takes longer to warm up than most, and I was just waiting and waiting for that time when they'd start appearing in the edge. It seemed to take a long time and nothing was happening – nothing was being caught. There were a few people coming and going, but a lot of the time, as I said before, I was there on my own. Sometimes there were other people there, and I've got to say that this year the people who I was bumping into were a great bunch of blokes – really nice. There were a lot of good people in the past, but this year in particular, they were the best of the bunch to be bumping into down there, in between hiding under bushes and whatever.

It was good, but I was just waiting for that period when it warmed up enough. I was keeping certain spots baited up, as there were so many spots where I expected fish to come and feed. It's got more difficult over the years definitely; I've spoken to people who have fished it in the past, going back seven, eight or nine years, and they said you could get five or six spots going around the lake in the margins. You'd go round and think, oh there's mid-30 feeding there and there's a 20lb common there. But you know, these people were looking for The Black Mirror, so they were often leaving those spots and just putting more bait in, but you could probably get half a dozen spots going if you did it properly, whereas now, you're lucky if you find one or two – it's difficult to find spots where they will feed. To give you an idea what it was like, going back to that first spot where I got a bite after about nine nights, that was in 2006, and to this day, I don't think a fish has ever visited that spot again. I always carried on looking at it just for sentimental reasons, just because I'd had a bite there, but a bait never ever got touched again, so that's what you're up against.

I kept baiting and baiting a couple of other spots that I did sort of feel confident they would come back to, but the bait stayed there and the weed was gradually growing on them. It was a little bit hard to keep the confidence going on those spots because they just weeded over, and it looked like nothing was ever going to happen on them. It was just down to the weather really, the cold winter. The weed was starting to get a grip, but the water wasn't really warm enough for the fish to find those spots. But eventually one day, the bait was gone, a lot of the weed had been ripped up, and there was an opportunity. All of a sudden, it was starting to happen. There was no sign of any fish, so I put more bait on the spot, left it alone, and as it warmed up, the fish came into the edge. There was one certain overhanging tree, and I looked in it, and for the first time there were fish sitting in amongst the branches. The bait had gone once or twice, but I hadn't seen any fish, and then all of a sudden there were about half a dozen fish there. There was The Fat Common, which I'd caught the year before, another one that looked about the same size or maybe a little bit bigger, a couple of smaller commons, and every now and then The Black Mirror was coming in as well. The bait was gone that I'd put in there the night before, and I looked at those fish and thought, one of you is in trouble tonight; I knew one of them was going to make a mistake. It was such a confined little area; no one else bothered looking at it, and probably they wouldn't fancy fishing it. It was one of the spots that I'd found myself, which makes it all the more pleasing really because I hadn't followed anyone else, and I'd got something going.

Anyway that night I dropped a bait in there and I think it was about 2am that I got the bite. First of all I thought it was a tench; there was no resistance on the end, just a little flap of a tail on the top. I thought I'd ruined the spot for a tench, so I put the rod down, got my head torch out, looked down in the edge, and there was this common lying there. Of course I picked the rod up a bit sharpish, and it wouldn't go in the net. I thought, why won't it go in the net, and as it turned on its side, I saw it was The Fat Common again with a great big gut hanging over the edge. I should have been over the moon, but I was a little bit disappointed because I'd caught that fish before, and of all the fish that were coming and going in that tree, that was the last one I wanted to catch really. It was down in weight as well at 34lb 2oz, but you know, it was a Mere carp, the first one of the year, and the biggest anyway. I expected that to be the end of that spot as well, as generally speaking once you'd had a take and fish had disturbed the spot, they didn't often come back. That could have been it for the year on that spot, but I was still going to keep baiting it up anyway – there was no harm in putting a bit of bait in there just to see what happened. It did dry up there for quite a while, and nothing was happening. I kept putting bait in there, but it would just float up to the top. The weed gradually started to come back a little bit, and the water started to colour up as well, going green again, so the visibility was bad.

It was a few weeks later, probably late May I suppose, that I saw three fish in the bay – two commons and The Black Mirror. Most of the bait was still there but there was one little area, a little 3ft hole in the weed that had been cleaned. I was still in two minds about fishing that way for The Black Mirror, because most of the past captures had been from open water. The other thing was that The Black Mirror had never actually been caught at that end of the lake in the spring or the early part of the year. Tel had it up that end of the lake off The Beach, Dave Lane had caught it from The Canopy on the other side, and Si Baker had caught it off The Beach, but they were all later in the year. All the spring captures had all been down the other end, so I always had it in my mind that I should be fishing down that end in the open water spots. Then at the same time I was thinking to myself, well The Black Mirror's here and my bait's been going in the edge … It might have been a little common eating the baits, you know, but with all those things swirling round in your mind, you've just got to go with your instincts.

I lowered my bait on the spot again, down in about 8ft of water, and I could see it on the bottom. Through the night nothing happened and I thought, that's another chance missed. It got to about 7am, and I was virtually right on the path, so I thought, I've got to get myself out of the way here. I took my bits and pieces and put them right back in the undergrowth in the bushes, and just lay down, trying to catch up on a little bit of kip, just with my sounder box. I must have dozed off, as next thing there was just this one toner from my sounder box. To get to the rod, I literally I had to jump in the lake, wade through the water, over a tree stump, and grab the rod. Because of the angle that I was fishing, I had to walk another 20yds along the reeds up to my chest in water just to get clear of the branches, and all the time, the spool was just whizzing round.

I was wondering which fish it was because when I caught The Fat Common earlier, The Black Mirror was the last fish to be seen in those branches the evening before, so I'd been fairly close there. This time there were three fish in the bay and The Black Mirror was one of them, so I had a one in three chance, and I was thinking to myself, this could really be it! It had stormed off out, but thankfully I'd dipped the rod tip right down under the branches, and the line came up clear, just going out in the middle of the bay, and I thought, that's the first job out of the way. It fought really hard and although the water is quite clear, I couldn't actually see which fish it was because of the angle from where I was in the water. It was a good old battle, and as it came up I thought, oh, it's a common, and I was a little bit disappointed. But then I actually saw which it was, and it was a cracking fish, one of the originals, and actually the first fish Terry Hearn caught out of the lake. I'd read that chapter from his book so many times – one of the best chapters that's ever been written I should think – and I always looked at that picture and thought, that is one fish I'd love to catch and there it was in my net.

I mean it hasn't changed much either; it was 32lb 4oz, so it's only a couple of pounds bigger than when Terry caught it 15 years earlier. I was well pleased with that one in the end, even though I knew I'd been close to The Black Mirror. So that was two captures where The Black Mirror had been in the area, so it was boosting my confidence. I was thinking other people are fishing off round the lake and they haven't seen The Black Mirror,

My biggest Mere common, The Fat One, which I caught twice, but at 38lb 4oz here.

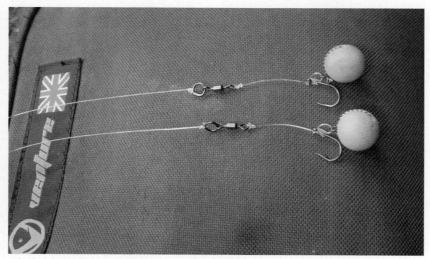

The hinged stiff rig caught me a couple of Mere carp.

It was the margin fishing, which always interested me most, and in the end was the downfall of most of my Mere captures.

One of my most pleasing captures was this original common, which had been Tel's first fish from the lake all those years ago.

but I've seen it, and I've been close to it, so I'm doing things right. Bt the same time, just the reputation of that fish was getting to me. I kept saying to myself, it's only a carp, and if it was in another lake it would probably get caught more. If it was called something else and lived in another lake, I would have caught it by now, but because it's The Black Mirror you think, I'm never going to catch this fish. It was funny; you started off the tape by saying, "I knew you'd catch it," and it's amazing the amount of people who said that to me. But of course when you're down there trying and it's not happening… You probably had the same with Bazil I'm sure; you think, well it's alright for you saying that, but I'm here doing my nut and it ain't happening – other people are catching it, and I'm close, but I could be here another ten years being close.

You do go through all the emotions, wondering if you're ever going to catch this fish, and I found myself sitting there sometimes just looking at the lake saying, "Look, just let me catch it, just let me catch it and go – I'll leave you alone." I did all sorts of things; I used to go down there in the winter and clear up rubbish and things, just to say, "I'm doing you a favour here, lake, so do me one." In a way that probably helped me, and everyone else, with the fishing anyway, because it's a little bit like Cassien when you

For the margins I always fished a fairly basic rig with a Solar Club Mix bottom bait.

weren't allowed to night fish. If you're making a nuisance of yourself, people are seeing you and there's rubbish everywhere, then obviously it's going to be noticed, but out of sight out of mind, sort of thing. I made a conscious decision to keep the place clean and respect the place, and maybe it did help with the authorities. They looked at it at different times, and thought, oh well, can't see anyone, and there's no rubbish, so maybe they did leave it alone a little bit. I was just trying to pay the lake back, as I enjoyed it so much, but it just seemed like it was never going to happen.

When it did happen, it was so weird; it was totally different to all the other fishing I'd done there. The World Cup was on, England was playing that evening, and a couple of people said, "Are you going to watch the match?" I said, "You've got to be joking; I've got to be somewhere else." The weather wasn't brilliant for it or anything; it was blowing a northerly, and it wasn't very warm. I got down there about 3.30, and the first job is to make sure you get a reasonable spot. I was thinking to myself that The Beach was probably a good area on a northerly. I went straight in there, as there was no one in The Beach, obviously. I couldn't see anyone else on there at all; they were all at home watching the football, so I dumped the gear in The Beach. The next job was to check the baited areas. There were two areas I'd baited when I'd left two days earlier on June 16th; one was my spot where I caught the two other fish and one was further down the lake. The one where I caught the two other fish was closest, so I went straight to that spot first, and there was a common on the bait, on this little area that was only 3ft wide. I looked down and there was this tail waving, and I knew which fish it was; it was the one they call The Twisty Common, again one of the old original fish. It's not the biggest in there, around high 20's, but it's one of the fish I wanted to catch, so I thought, right, that'll do nicely.

I legged it back and got a rod out. I only had my stiff rigs on at the time, but I knew I had an old bottom bait rig in my bag, so I put that on straight away with a 14mm Club Mix boilie. I went back and the bait was gone, but the fish was gone as well. I thought, perfect, and just lowered it onto the spot. I stepped back, and I think I was just about to send Joan a text saying that it looked good, and that I might get one in the morning, and I'd literally just got the phone out my pocket, and there was a one-toner. The bait had been in the water a minute, and that was it; the phone got launched in the brambles, and the trousers got ripped off because I had to jump in the lake again. I jumped in the lake, grabbed the rod, waded 20yds along the reeds as I did before, and hoped and prayed that the line wasn't caught round the branches. I dipped the rod down and the line came up free again, out in the middle of the bay. It had weeded itself up so I got myself in position. I wasn't too worried about the weed; I knew I could get the fish out because it was The Twisty Common I was playing.

I pulled into it and nothing happened, so I tightened down and pulled harder than I wanted to... You know when you pull and you think, oh, I'm giving it more than I want to give it here and I don't like it, but then all of a sudden I felt a movement and the fish came free. I could feel the head rocking, gained probably about 10-15yds of line, and as I was winding, a couple of reeds got caught in the bale arm and jammed the reel. I pulled them out, but by the time I'd got contact again, the fish was weeded again. So I went through the same process; I got it out of the weed, and again, because of the angle from where I was in the water, and because it was quite overcast, I couldn't see the fish. But I just remember as it rolled, I saw this head and shoulders facing me and I thought, it's bigger than I was expecting, but I was still thinking I was playing the common, because I hadn't seen anything else there.

I had it under control, got the net in, and as the fish came up it turned on its side just as it went over the drawstring, and I looked and I thought, that's a mirror... I knew which one it was, because there are only two in there, a 30lb'er and The Black Mirror, and I knew it was too big to be anything else. I just launched the rod over my shoulder, dived in the landing net and grabbed the wrist to look at that flat lobe, and sure enough there it was. The next bit was just a blur; I was jumping up and down all on my own, shouting, "I've got it, I've got it, I've done it!" I'd only been there 15 minutes, which was mad after all those days and all those nights. All that time I'd been there and then when it happened it was all so simple, just as easy as anything else. It was just being in the right place at right time – one of those windows of opportunity. 15 minutes earlier there might have been nothing there and all the bait would have been still been there, and 15 minutes later... It was just meant to happen that time and it did happen, and there it was, The Black Mirror, the greatest fish in England, I think. A lot of people think it's the greatest fish in England too, and just to see it in my landing net was amazing, absolutely amazing.

The first thing I did was to phone Joan up. There was no one there, and I wasn't going to photograph it myself on the self-timer or whatever, so there were a million thoughts going through my head. I phoned Joan up and she wasn't feeling too well, but the first thing she said was, "Right, I'm going to be down there in five minutes." I thought, oh right, sorted, that's perfect, because all of the fishing I did on The Mere was very personal, and most of the time I did it on my own, so it was a personal capture. I didn't want loads of people if you know what I mean, so it was nice that just Joan

The magnificent Black Mirror, England's finest carp, and the end of my quest.